Six Primroses Each

&

Other Plays for Young Actors

by

Ellen Dryden

FIRST WRITES

First Writes Books
Norfolk 2009

First Writes Books. Norfolk 2009

First Writes Books are published by:-
First Writes Theatre Company Ltd.
Lime Kiln Cottage, High Starlings,
Banham, Norfolk NR16 2BS.

Printed by The Morris Printing Co.
57-61 Pitt Street, Norwich NR3 1DE.

© Ellen Dryden 2000
   First published 2000
   Reprinted 2001
   Reprinted 2004
   Reprinted 2009

ISBN 9781901071016

These plays are fully protected by copyright.
All requests for professional performance must be addressed to:-
First Writes Theatre Company Ltd.
Lime Kiln Cottage, High Starlings,
Banham, Norfolk NR16 2BS.

Rights of performance by amateurs are controlled by:-
Samuel French Ltd.
52 Fitzroy Street,
London W1T 5JR
and they, or their authorised agents, issue licences to amateurs on payment of a fee.
It is an infringement of the Copyright to give any performance or public reading of the play before the fee has been paid and the licence issued

The Royalty Fee is subject to contract and subject to variation at the sole discretion of Samuel French Ltd.

CONTENTS

	Page
Introduction	1

PLAYS

SIX PRIMROSES EACH	5
ADVENTURE CAMP	19
THE CHILDREN'S WARD	37
THE PRESS GANG	53
IN SERVICE	73
THE COLOUR OF COMPASSION	89
THE STRAWBERRY TEA	115
FLATMATES	131
SHADOWS	153

MONOLOGUES

HALLO, IS THAT YOU?	161
MADAM HAS A COMBINATION SKIN	166

For

the actors, directors, technicians

and workers, backstage and front of house,

of

CHISWICK YOUTH THEATRE

who

gave the first performances of these plays.

Writing for Young actors

The plays in this volume were written by Ellen Dryden, for the use of Chiswick Youth Theatre, and they were in regular workshop and performance use by young actors between the ages of eleven and eighteen.

Chiswick Youth Theatre was an organization run by theatre professionals in their spare time, based at Chiswick Community School. It catered for young people of a wide range of ages and abilities, and attempted to give them some experience of all kinds of theatre in regular public performance up to the highest standard. Shakespeare, Ibsen, Pinero, Kaufman and Hart and Peter Whelan were among the writers performed by CYT, but new plays, both improvised and scripted, were also a regular part of the diet.

Full scale new plays and musicals were presented by CYT - Don Taylor's **Daughters of Venice** and **Women of Athens,** and the Dryden/Taylor/Young musicals, **The Burston Drum** and **Summer in the Park.** But in addition, the playwrights who worked with CYT felt the need to create another kind of work, one act plays specially designed for young people, for both workshop and public performance. All the plays in this volume were publicly performed with great success by CYT, and were also in regular workshop use in CYT's weekly meetings. Working with them, young actors learned how to move, speak, take a cue, build a character and create a theatrical climax by working with fellow actors. These plays contain the basic building blocks of theatre, in both acting and presentation, which is why CYT kept them in continuous use. Several school generations of young players cut their dramatic teeth on these plays before moving on to perform in larger scale works. As a matter of record, both **The Children's Ward** and **The Press Gang** were written and performed before the television series of the same names were transmitted.

One of the most useful things Ellen Dryden has done in these pieces is to write a series of plays which covers the whole age range of secondary education, with good parts and dramatic situations for everyone, from First Years to Sixth Formers or students. Broadly speaking, the plays are suited to different stages of school life – **Flatmates, The Strawberry Tea, Shadows** and the monologues for the older pupils, **Six Primroses Each** and **Adventure Camp** for Key Stage 3, **The Children's Ward, In Service** and **The Press Gang** for Key Stage 4. But the scheme is flexible and was manipulated in all directions by the young actors of CYT, who often delighted in playing above, or below, their own ages.

Perhaps the most striking thing about young actors in their early teen years is the vividness of their imagination. This often expresses itself in compelling and original improvisations, which, by their nature, tend to be limited in subject matter to the worlds that young people know and inhabit: so that most of their improvisations are thinly disguised versions of the conflicts and fantasies of their own lives - relationships with parents, the opposite sex, bullying, etc. etc. In our experience, they want other things from adult dramatists: not an attempt to mimic their lives, which they know better than we do, but the creation of new worlds for them to explore. So many discoveries are being made, and the world of the creative imagination is being entered for the first time, so that the inhabiting of imaginary landscapes is particularly attractive and satisfying for them. To set plays in periods from the past - World War Two, the Victorian Age, the Seventies - or in worlds known but not yet experienced - a children's ward, a students' house, an empty theatre - adds a degree of excitement that our young actors found stimulating. When these plays do enter the world of the contemporary young, they treat subjects less likely to arise from improvisations - the strangeness of old age and death, the fragility and difficulty of relationships, and the cruelties people inflict upon each other as they try to find space for themselves.

One play in this volume, **The Colour of Compassion**, was created in quite a different way. In a workshop situation, Ellen Dryden introduced a group of younger actors to the story of Mary Seacole, the nurse from the Caribbean, who, having been rejected by the English establishment because of her colour, went to nurse soldiers in the Crimean War under her own steam, and became a national heroine. Together the group read passages from Mary Seacole's autobiography, and improvised scenes, so that a play began to emerge. The characters were created to suit the people available. The part of the silent man, for instance, was created for a boy who wanted to take part but did not wish to speak.

Ellen Dryden took notes during these rehearsals and then wrote the play, based upon the structure and dialogue the young actors had themselves created, as well as Mary Seacole's own words. In one scene, Mary, trying to board a ship, was taunted by some American women, using the now most unacceptable racist word. The young black actress who played Mary insisted that the word should be part of the performance, and it was played to an audience of parents and friends. We have replaced it in this published version, not wishing to give offence to some who have not made the decision our actress made. Those who wish to perform what was actually said to Mary trying to board an American steamboat, will find the reference in her autobiography, **The Wonderful Adventures of Mrs Mary Seacole in Many Lands**.

Finally, it is quality of play writing that matters, and it is Ellen Dryden's achievement in these short plays and monologues to have created fully adult dramas that young players want to act, and which their parents and friends enjoy seeing performed. Much of the subject matter of these plays is profoundly disturbing: the playwright pulls no punches, and without resorting to violence or language unacceptable in the classroom or youth theatre, pictures some of the darkness and uncertainty of growing up, the pain of entering the adult world. There is wit and humour too, and plenty of laughter in performance, but this is no comforting picture of the world of young people. Her characters confront the death of their contemporaries and old people, social division, class rivalries and simple personal cruelty in ways which the young players who perform them recognise to be true. This is perhaps the secret of the success of these plays. The young actors like playing them because they know that they are being initiated into the world as adults see it, and being required, by the exercise of their imaginations to enter it themselves. They are not being talked down to, but being invited, by a working writer, to join her and enter into the serious and exhilarating process of making theatre.

Don Taylor 2000.

SIX PRIMROSES EACH

CHARACTERS

PAULINE

RICHARD

DAVID

PAUL

RAYMOND

ROSEMARY

LILLIAN

ANGELA

JANET

VOICE (OFFSTAGE)

MISS DEACON

The play is set in a Church Hall in 1940.

SIX PRIMROSES EACH

We hear being played very sweetly and simply on the piano the children's hymn, **Tell me the stories of Jesus.** *We are in a bleak, empty Sunday Schoolroom. There are a few chairs lined up in rows and a text on the wall, 'Suffer the little children to come unto me, and forbid them not.'*

Pauline and Richard come in, warily. Richard is a small, inward-looking boy, who scuttles about as if wanting not to be seen. Pauline, his sister, is fiercely protective. They are followed by David, a tall, lounging, aggressive boy who hits out first and asks questions later; Raymond, a nervous, worried boy; Rosemary and Lillian, two self-assured girls, friends who keep apart from the rest; and finally Paul, a wiry, restless boy who conceals his fears by being extra noisy. They are all wearing labels with their names on. Richard goes to sit down on a chair downstage.

PAULINE: No. Don't sit down Richard.

RICHARD: I'm tired. Why can't I? I want to sit down.

PAULINE: (*With a look at the others*) Well, she never said we could.

DAVID: (*Sitting down and stretching out*) Huh! You don't want to take any notice of her!

PAUL: (*Joining him*) No! Stuck up old cow!

PAULINE: Don't swear.

PAUL: Cow's not swearing.

PAULINE: Well, it's not very nice - you shouldn't go round saying things like that about people you don't know.

RAYMOND: Well - I... I... didn't think *she* seemed very nice... When she couldn't say my name... she... she-

PAUL: Nobody can say your name!

RAYMOND: That's no call to... to just laugh and say 'Oh well, we'll have to call you Raymond Kay then.' And look, she's wrote 'Raymond Kay' on this label.

He twists his label round and looks at it worriedly.

7

PAULINE: Well that's your fault. You shouldn't have gone and lost your proper label in the first place. I bet you was chewing it!

RAYMOND: I didn't!... It come off! I don't know where it went.

PAUL: It don't matter.

RAYMOND: Yes it does. If they go giving me another name my Mum won't know where I am. She won't think it's me!

Richard has moved to sit down. Pauline snaps at him, irritably.

PAULINE: Richard! Stop it! Come here. You've got to stay with me! They promised Mum they wouldn't split us up. If you go wandering off they might! You stay with me here by the door.

PAUL: (*Nastily*) Yeah, go on, Pauline Abbott, stop by the door so you're first in the queue. 'Please Miss, I'm Pauline Abbott. Abbott's first on the register, Miss. This is my brother, Miss. Can we be first, Miss?'

PAULINE: Shut up, you! If they try to put us with you I'll tell them about you. I bet you wet the bed! I'll tell them about the time you wet yourself in class when Mr Greenlaw wouldn't let you be excused!

The others all laugh at Paul.

PAUL: That was in the Infants. Years ago! Anyway, I did it on purpose to get old Greenlaw. He got in more trouble about that than I did. My Dad come up the school and complained.

DAVID: Go on. He never!

PAUL: Yes he did!

DAVID: Your Dad's too scared. Got out of going in the Army, didn't he?

PAUL: He wasn't allowed. He'd got to stop in the Docks. Anyway, you haven't even got a Dad!

DAVID: Yes I have. He's away. Fighting. In the Army.

PAUL: Where?

DAVID: Shows how much you know. You're not allowed to say. It's secret.

ROSEMARY: Your Dad's not in the Army. You haven't got a Dad. You've never had a Dad. You didn't have a Dad before the War!

LILLIAN: Yeah! His Mum's a tart.

DAVID: I'll thump you, Willby!

LILLIAN: Go on then!

DAVID: I don't hit girls. I might kill you.

PAUL: She might hit you back you mean!

PAULINE: Oh shut up the lot of you! You get on my nerves!

There is a pause. They look round.

LILLIAN: Why have they put us in here?

DAVID: 'Cos we're all from the same school, stupid! We'll have to go to school together down here. Well, you will. I'm not stopping.

PAULINE: You've got to. You've got no say. We've been evacuated here and we've got to stop here until somebody fetches us back.

ROSEMARY: My Nan says it'll be lovely. Like a long holiday. She went on a holiday to the country when she was at school. She said it was smashing. They fed the chickens and fetched the eggs and everything.

DAVID: I ain't picking no eggs.

PAULINE: You don't pick eggs, clever! You... fetch 'em.

DAVID: You can do what you like with them! I'm not stopping. Soon as I've gone to wherever it is they've put me, I shall wait till it's dark and then climb out of the window and leg it back to London.

LILLIAN: You can't do that! It's took all day to get here on the train and the bus. It's miles.

DAVID: I can sleep rough.

ROSEMARY: What about food?

DAVID: Well, I'll stick a load of stuff in my pockets at tea-time.

LILLIAN: They might not give you any.

PAUL: They have to. When you're an evacuee they have to look after you. And feed you. And send you back in the same condition they got you in!

DAVID: Anyway, I've got a ten-bob note in my sock!

PAUL: You haven't!

DAVID: Yes I have.

PAUL: I don't believe you. Let's have a look.

DAVID: All right.

He pulls his sock down a fraction, revealing a small piece of paper.

PAULINE: That's not a ten-bob note.

DAVID: Yes it is.

PAULINE: Take it out and show us properly.

DAVID: No fear! Wouldn't trust you lot.

PAUL: Where'd you get it from then?

DAVID: Pinched it.

PAUL: Where from?

DAVID: That's my business.

PAULINE: I think it's a bit of rolled up newspaper.

LILLIAN: Yes it's newspaper. 'Cos he's got great big holes in his socks and his Mum don't bother to mend 'em!

ROSEMARY: And he smells!

They retreat in disgust.

RAYMOND: I'll have to tell them what my proper name is. They've got to get it right. They might have it down wrong on all the lists. It's quite easy when you know. Do you think I should go in there and tell that lady how to say it?

LILLIAN: No. She told us to stop in here. She'd shout at you.

ROSEMARY: Yes. She didn't half shout at that little black-haired kid that had lost her bag.

RICHARD: Pauline. I want to go home now. I don't like it here. Let's go home.

There is a moment's pause. This is how they all feel, but cannot admit to their fear and misery.

PAULINE: (*Sadly*) It's all right Richard. You're with me. I'll look after you. Like I promised Mum...

RICHARD: I don't like it here. Let's go back.

PAULINE: We can't go back, lovey. There's no trains...

RICHARD: Well, Mum can come and get us. I don't want to stay here.

Pauline bites her lip and puts her arm round him and strokes his hair mechanically. She sighs.

DAVID: You can come back with me. I'll take him.

PAULINE: (*Flaring up*) I wouldn't let you take him to the next room, David Fawley! And you can shut up about going back home and upsetting everybody. You're just a big mouth! It's all right, Richie love, I won't let them upset you. We're going to go and stop in a nice place - just you and me, - and we'll have a lovely little room all to ourselves and Mum'll come and see us and we'll go for a nice walk, and then -

She breaks off.

DAVID: Who do you think's gonna want him!

He gestures to Richard, who is sitting head down, and shoulders hunched, looking the picture of misery.

PAULINE: You shut up or I'll smash your face in.

ROSEMARY: I don't like the way they've just left us in here. All the others off the train are in there. They might forget about us. We've been here ages.

PAUL: No we haven't. Not as long as on Ealing Station.

ROSEMARY: I wish I was on Ealing Station now. Going the other way.

LILLIAN: Do you think they'll let us be together, Rose?

ROSEMARY: I dunno, Lil. We could say we were sisters.

RAYMOND: No. You've got different names.

ROSEMARY: Cousins then.

RAYMOND: Cousins don't count.

The door opens and Angela and Janet burst in. Angela is a self-confident, bouncy, Manchester girl. Janet is her side-kick, a quiet, concealed kind of girl, a little better spoken than the others - suburban rather than East End London. She is totally under Angela's thumb.

ANGELA: Oh, hello! I didn't know there was anybody in here! (*Of course she did. That's why she's come in*) They must have forgotten about you.

She looks them up and down.

I'm not surprised, eh Janet?

JANET: (*Giggling*) No.

ANGELA: I don't think you ought to sit on the chairs. Not till you've been disinfected!

PAULINE: Don't you be so cheeky! Who do you think you are?

ROSEMARY: Did they tell you to come here and wait with us?

ANGELA: No! I'm not an *evacuee*! I'm here with my Auntie Joan to pick out a couple of you. She's in there talking to Miss Deacon. They probably put you in here 'cos they think you've got nits. Or fleas. (*Janet giggles*) Or ringworm or something like that!

ROSEMARY: What's ringworm?

ANGELA: It's something dirty people get. Your hair all comes out in little round patches. A lot of the scruffy lot from London get it. They paint your head purple.

JANET: No that's impetigo, Angela.

ANGELA: (*Airily*) And ringworm.

LILLIAN: (*Outraged*) Well none of us've got that. Well the boys might have... Did you say you wanted two together? 'Cos me and Rosemary - my friend - we wanted to be together.

PAULINE: And nobody's going to separate me and my brother Richard.

ANGELA: (*Looking Pauline up and down*) You'll not have much say. You go in and stand there and the people from the village walk round and look at you and say 'I'll have that one - it looks quite clean. Is it house-trained?' And if they don't like the look of you, they don't take you and you have to go to the Vicar's. I picked Janet, didn't I?

JANET: Yes. I was all by myself. Angela and her Auntie –

ANGELA: I'm just stopping with my Auntie while the bombing's on. She's got a big house up in the woods. She's my Mom's sister. And she can take two more.

ROSEMARY: Where do you live then?

ANGELA: Manchester.

PAUL: Manchester! There ain't no bombs in Manchester! What would they want to go and bomb Manchester for when they could bomb London?

DAVID: There's nothing in Manchester worth bombing! Not like the East End. You should see the Docks go up. I was down my Gran's the first time they come. Fires everywhere all over the road. It was like daylight... it was so bright. Great big vats of whisky blowing up - and petrol and smoke and buildings falling down.

PAUL: Yeah! The old woman next door to us she got buried alive with her cat and her budgie. And when they dug her out, she was stone dead! And the budgie and the cat was still alive!

DAVID: And they bombed the United Dairies down our way,- the stables. And all the 'orses was in there. And when we went to school the next day there was little bits of dead 'orse all over the road - for miles!

RICHARD: (*Desperately*) I want to go home. I want to go back home. I don't want to stay here. Take me back home now, Pauline...

He shakes his head desperately and puts his face in his hands.

PAULINE: Oh now look what you've done! (*Paul and David shrug*) It's all right, Richard. I'm here. Pauline's here.

ANGELA: (*Regarding Richard with distaste*) How old is he?

PAULINE: What's that got to do with you? He's eleven.

ANGELA: He's only ten pence in the shilling in't he?

PAULINE: What are you talking about?

ANGELA: He's gormless! He's norr'all there!

PAULINE: Yes he is. There's nothing wrong with him. He's just got bad nerves! From all the air-raids. He gets upset.

DAVID: (*Cruelly mocking*) And he's - stoopid - as well.

Pauline swings round and thumps him.

PAULINE: Leave him alone!!!

ROSEMARY: Oh stop it, Pauline. I wish you'd run away now, David Fawley. Up the fast line! Look if we start fighting they won't want us!

ANGELA: I expect they're saving you for Mrs Fitz-Hughes at the Manor. She always takes a load of scruffy ones. They never stay long though! She's got a row of little camp beds in the stables and she makes the evacuees do all the work. Scrub the floors, clean out the pigsties, muck out the hens and black-lead all the grates. And if she has Catholics she makes them eat meat on Fridays, and she made David Goldberg eat a pig's brains - and he was sick all over and she sent him back.

JANET: And she gives you bread and milk all the time. With stale bread, and she waters the milk. And no sugar. And the Major - that's her husband - he's too old to be a proper soldier - he lets you go on nature walks on his land. And he says you can pick primroses. 'The children can pick six each with one leaf, and the Teachers can pick twelve with two leaves.' And it's freezing...

PAUL: Do you have to go for walks?

ANGELA: Yeah! All through the mud. And you have to go to Church on Sunday. Or Chapel.

JANET: That's only if you're with Mrs Fitz-Hughes.

ANGELA: It's dead funny in Chapel. My Auntie Joan goes. And the man next door hates the Chapel, and he killed his pig on a Sunday morning! We were just singing the first hymn when it started squealing its head off 'cos it knew what he was going to do, and he chased it all round the garden and it squealed and squealed and then it was quiet - and everybody looked at each other 'cos they knew he'd cut its throat and it was bleeding to death.

A voice is heard from outside. Everyone freezes at the sound of authority, except for Angela and Janet.

VOICE: Angela... Janet, where are you? Angela lovey... Come along.

ANGELA: Oh that's my Auntie Joan! Come on Janet. Well I shouldn't think I'll see you lot again. (*With pride*) And it just so happens that Manchester is a very important industrial city - with Docks and the Ship Canal. It's just as important as rotten old London!

DAVID: Well if you like it so much why don't you go back there? They might manage to drop a bomb on you!

ROSEMARY: If you could put in a word for me and Lillian?

LILLIAN: Shut up, Rose...

ANGELA: I might. I'm not promising though. I don't know whether Auntie Joan would want smelly Londoners in the house. Come on, Janet.

She and Janet go out. Pauline sticks her tongue out after her.

RAYMOND: Oh. I should have given her a note to give that woman about my name.

A harassed-looking woman enters with a collection of lists.

MISS DEACON: Ah good. Now listen carefully please, children. I am Miss Deacon. You are going to be allocated to billeters in a moment.

The four children, who speak to her, all speak at once.

RAYMOND: This label is wrong, Miss. I'm not Raymond Kay.

PAULINE: I mustn't be separated from Richard.

ROSEMARY: I want to be with Lillian.

LILLIAN: Me and Rosemary are best friends.

MISS DEACON: Please! Please! Please be quiet!!! We can't get anywhere with all this noise! Now please be quiet. Listen to what I have to say. Line up by the door as I call out your names. Girls first. Pauline Abbott.

PAULINE: Please Miss, he's my brother. He's got to be with me, Miss.

MISS DEACON: Pauline Abbott. Did you hear what I said? Did you?

PAULINE: Yes, Miss.

MISS DEACON: Well please do as you are told! We won't get anywhere if you mess about like this. It's going to be difficult enough as it is to place all of you. All the girls. Over to the door as I call your names. You first.

Pauline goes reluctantly upstage.

RICHARD: Pauline - I want to go home.

PAULINE: *(Anguished)* Sshh!! It'll be all right. Don't fret. Please.

MISS DEACON: Rosemary Baker.

ROSEMARY: Here, Miss.

She wins a slight smile from Miss Deacon as she scurries up to the door.

MISS DEACON: Lillian Willby.

LILLIAN: Yes, Miss.

She joins Rosemary. They whisper surreptitiously, at the door.

MISS DEACON: Right girls. You can go in and line up with the other girls on the far side of the Hall by the piano. Off you go.

The girls go out, Pauline looking despairingly at Richard.

MISS DEACON: Now the boys. Richard Abbott.

RICHARD: I don't like it here. I want to go home. Where's Pauline?

MISS DEACON: That'll do. Stop whining, you've only just got here! Goodness, anybody would think we were all ogres!! Paul Cross.

PAUL: Yes Miss.

MISS DEACON: By the door. Like the girls. Jump to it.

PAUL: *(To Richard)* Come on. I'll take you to Pauline.

He and Richard go to the door.

MISS DEACON: David Fawley. Oh...

She pauses and reads a special note on her list.

Oh yes... just a minute, David... ermm... You'd better wait here till I see... There's a bit of a problem about your medical form. (*Brightly*) Not to worry. I'm sure it'll be all right. We'll have to see. You just sit here and I'll sort it out in two ticks.

DAVID: Ain't I going with the others then, Miss?

MISS DEACON: Probably. I've just got to see to a couple of things. Just sit down, David. Raymond Kay.

David reluctantly sits down.

RAYMOND: Miss, it isn't Kay. My name. It isn't Kay.

MISS DEACON: Well that's what I've got here. And that's what your label says.

RAYMOND: It isn't my label, Miss.

MISS DEACON: Don't be silly. Whose label is it then?

RAYMOND: Mine, Miss. But the name's wrong. It should be Kashelevitsky.

MISS DEACON: Good heavens, what a mouthful! Let's settle for Kay for the time being shall we? Off you go.

RAYMOND: But, Miss, I can't have the wrong name...

MISS DEACON: Don't be silly. We haven't got any other Raymond Kays, have we? We're not going to muddle you up! Off you go now, boys. Not you, David. Line up in the Hall. Opposite the girls. Quick march!

The boys go out, casting serious looks at David. Miss Deacon puts her head in her hands.

MISS DEACON: Phew...

DAVID: (*Getting up and crossing to Miss Deacon*) There's nothing wrong with me, Miss. Honest!

MISS DEACON: I've told you we'll have it all sorted out in a jiffy! But you may have to have a camp bed here tonight. Just for tonight. But don't worry. Wait here. I'll be back soon.

She goes out leaving David alone.

DAVID: I'm not sleeping on no rotten camp bed. I'm not stopping here to be pushed around. There's nothing the matter with me. I'm not staying in no stinking country with stinking pigs and stinking old cows! I'm legging it back to London. I'm not scared of a few bombs. I'll climb out of the window and hop it off home. Yeah. That's what I'll do.

He stays quite still. Fade out as the piano music is heard again, very soft and sweet.

THE END

ADVENTURE CAMP

CHARACTERS

KATE
ROSIE
LOTTIE
SOPHIE
TARA
TRACIE
EMMA
HELEN
ANNE
POLLY
JOANNE
DEBBIE

The play is set at an open-air adventure camp in the 1970s.

ADVENTURE CAMP

The stage is empty of all scenery except for a rough wooden table set centre stage. On it stands a couple of plastic washing up bowls and a large plastic water carrier. Ranged around it on the floor is an assortment of washing up, including some very large, very dirty saucepans, iron cooking pots and earthenware bowls.

Upstage centre is a stand-by tap. Downstage left and downstage right are two groups of girls. They are lying on sleeping bags or blankets, like two five- pointed stars, feet to the middle, as if in a large bell-tent.

In the tent downstage right are Tara, Emma, Lottie, Sophie and Tracie. In the tent downstage left are Helen, Joanne, Debbie, Polly and Anne.

Two girls are standing, washing up, at the table. Kate is washing and Rosie is drying with a filthy piece of rag. They are working very slowly, incompetently and unconvincingly. Kate is in a very bad mood.

KATE: (*In an affected voice*) 'Mummy was furious actually. She made them take it back at once and change it. I mean, it was Daddy's birthday present and you don't expect that sort of thing from Harrods.' (*In her own voice*) Silly cow!

ROSIE: Yeah... This cloth's soaked.

KATE: Her and her designer sleeping-bag. What's she here for anyway? Why isn't she in - Monte Carlo?

ROSIE: I dunno. She's not here to do any of the work I know that. I don't think it's fair. Somebody ought to tell Janice. We're all supposed to be mucking in. Do you know she just came out and looked at the scrambled egg pan and said 'Oh, what a mess! How are you going to get that off?' - and went!

KATE: Janice won't do anything. Too frightened of upsetting Mrs Telford lah-di-dah Jones.

ROSIE: What's it got to do with her?

KATE: Oh come on! You must have heard Lottie. (*Affected voice*) 'Of course it's a terrific secret. You mustn't tell a soul but Mummy and Daddy have given a whacking great donation to the Club for this holiday. They think it's such a frightfully good cause. You won't tell anybody will you?'

ROSIE: (*Giggling*). Cheek! I reckon Mumsie and Dadsie are in Monte Carlo and they've given the money to get rid of Lottie.

KATE: You could be right.

There is a pause as they glumly continue washing up

ROSIE: Where do you think they got these saucepans from?

KATE: I dunno. If they're going to feed us all this muck you'd think they'd get some decent, non-stick pans.

ROSIE: The food's awful isn't it?

KATE: Terrible. I don't eat porridge. It makes me sick.

ROSIE: Looks like sick, you mean. And me. When I went to the Isle of Wight last year we had proper food. Cornflakes, hamburgers, chips and things. They weren't very nice but they were better than this muck!

KATE: What about that stuff we had last night?

ROSIE: Vegetable stew. Ugh!

KATE: I wonder if there's a chip shop in the village.

ROSIE: Shouldn't think so. It won a prize for the most beautiful village or something. That sort of place never has any decent shops....

KATE: There used to be a school here. A boarding school. That old man was talking to Janice about it.

ROSIE: Him in the shorts? I don't think old men ought to wear shorts. It's disgusting. Did you see his horrible old knees? All knobbly and them scraggy legs... and all the hairs were grey! Yuk!

KATE: He's seventy-nine.

ROSIE: No! Well. There you are. Should be ashamed of himself.

KATE: What's for tea?

ROSIE: That rotten doorstep bread!... dunno. Tara and Emma and Sophie are doing the tea.

KATE: If Sophie stops crying long enough. Do you know I didn't get a wink of sleep last night - she was snuffling and snivelling all night.

ROSIE: Well you could move. Make Tracie sleep next to her.

KATE: Don't make any difference in these tents.

ROSIE: Where'd they get them from? They're not what I call tents.

KATE: They're ex-army tents, Joanne says. I reckon the army chucked 'em away.

ROSIE: You can get smashing tents nowadays. When they said we were going to sleep in tents I thought it'd be quite nice. When I went on holiday with Debbie they had a tent - it was like a palace. It had a lounge and a kitchen and three bedrooms. It was better than our house!

KATE: This is supposed to be an adventure holiday. Adventure! What's adventure about sleeping in a horrible, smelly old tent and digging holes in the ground for the toilets and living off disgusting muck cooked in dustbins!

She gestures disgustedly at the saucepans with her dishmop.

That old git's behind it all! He used to be the boss of this prison school here and he couldn't get anybody to go to it so he's started a prison camp holiday to make up for it... He told Janice everybody's too soft nowadays. Too much easy living!

ROSIE: Well. It's hard enough here.

KATE: He reckons it's good for you to suffer.

ROSIE: We're doing that all right. (*Pause*) I wish I hadn't come. I thought it'd be good with all you lot here. But what with sick porridge and Lottie... Why did you come?

KATE: Get out of me Mum's way. She's got a new boyfriend. 'You are going to call me Uncle Alan aren't you, Katie?'... 'No I'm not and my name's not Katie.'

ROSIE: (*Throwing down her dishcloth and looking at the pans*) That'll have to do. I'm not doing any more. Tracie and Helen can do the rest. (*Thoughtfully*) You know what I've been thinking? They said if the weather was bad we'd sleep in the House...

KATE: So ?

ROSIE: Well. It might be better than them tents. There must be beds indoors.

KATE: They've probably got iron spikes through 'em. Anyway the weather's fantastic - hasn't been any rain for weeks. They won't let us go indoors in this weather. That's only if it pours.

ROSIE: Let's go and have a look anyway.

KATE: We're not supposed to -

ROSIE: Who cares? Who'll see us? Everybody's having their 'rest'. That's another thing. Making us have a lie-down like kids in a Nursery.

KATE: You're supposed to meditate!

They both giggle.

Oh all right. But we'd better keep away from Janice's tent.

They go off upstage left.

The attention shifts to the downstage right. tent. Sophie gives a muffled sob. Lottie sits up.

LOTTIE: Sophie! Are you still crying?

SOPHIE: No. (*Pause*) What if I am?

LOTTIE: It's jolly boring.

SOPHIE: Well. You don't have to listen.

LOTTIE: It's pretty difficult not to. Anyway you're supposed to be here to enjoy yourself.

SOPHIE: Huh!

LOTTIE: A lot of people have put a lot of effort - and money - into this week. The least you can do is pull yourself together and have some fun. What did you come for?

SOPHIE: (*Sniffing*) My Mum said it would stop me being such a baby.

LOTTIE: Well there you are then. You'll have to snap out of it.

TARA: (*Sitting up*) Oh shut up, Lottie! I don't blame her crying her eyes out with you going on all the time. You can't bully people into enjoying themselves.

TRACIE: Can we get up yet?

EMMA: No. It's only quarter to.

TRACIE: Is that all? That's the longest quarter of an hour I've ever spent in my life. And this is the stupidest idea I've ever known. Resting after dinner -

LOTTIE: - Lunch -

TRACIE: - Why can't we just go out? -

LOTTIE: - You're not supposed to be talking either -

EMMA: You can't go out. They've got great big Rottweilers out there to bite your legs off if you do anything out of order.

TRACIE: It'd be all right to go and tell Janice Sophie's crying.

TARA: Sophie's been crying non-stop since Friday afternoon. It's Sunday now. If we haven't managed to stop her by now we're not going to, are we?

SOPHIE: Janice doesn't like me. When I paid my deposit to come here she said. 'Oh. Are you sure you want to go, Sophie?' And she made me sit all by myself in the coach.

TRACIE: That's because you're always sick all over everybody.

EMMA: I don't think Janice likes anybody much.

TARA: She doesn't have to like people. She just has to organize them. Anyway she's avoiding everybody now. Haven't you noticed? She knows this place is a dead mistake.

EMMA: Yes. It's not her fault though. Hitler makes the rules here.

TRACIE: I bet his school was terrible.

LOTTIE: It was quite famous actually. He had a lot of theories about bringing up children to be self-reliant and resourceful. They didn't have to go to lessons or anything unless they wanted to. But they had to chop wood and have cold baths and things.

There is a pause. The others exchange glances.

EMMA: (*Spitefully*). Did Mummy send you there then ?

There is a tense pause.

LOTTIE: (*Turning away*) No.

TRACIE: What's self-reliant about not going to lessons? Three-quarters of our class bunk the afternoon anyway and Mr Jarvis don't seem to think it's too brilliant.

EMMA: Yeah! Dean Wilson and Toby Morton wouldn't mind chopping up wood. They smashed up three chairs in our Maths lesson.

TRACIE: Who do you have for Maths?

EMMA: Mr Hicks.

TRACIE: Oh. Yeah. Well, they would then.

EMMA: That's another thing. Where's all the boys?

TARA: Three fields away. (*She giggles*) Janice says because of certain 'unfortunate occurrences' during the latter years of his school Hitler became of the opinion that 'strict segregation was desirable.' - although it was against his principles really.

SOPHIE: What do you mean?

The others giggle. Sophie looks defiantly at them, and threatens to start crying again.

TARA: (*With heavy sarcasm*) I expect the boys made the girls cry!

SOPHIE: (*Whining*) Why can't we sleep in the house? I didn't know we were going to sleep in a field.

EMMA: Well, you didn't read your letter, did you?

SOPHIE: Anybody would think we were Guides –

TRACIE: Anyway the house is haunted. Three headless nuns wander round the battlements at full moon, wailing and waving their arms about.

SOPHIE: You're making it up. There aren't any battlements -

TRACIE: No I'm not. They're looking for girls to take away and turn into nuns. Because they had their heads chopped off for being nuns. So they have to make up the numbers.

LOTTIE: (*Muttering*) You got burned to death for religion - not beheaded

TRACIE: Well these didn't. They were beheaded.

She stares with dislike at Lottie.

LOTTIE: I - I - don't think you ought to tell stories like that. You'll only make Sophie worse.

There is a pause.

SOPHIE: What's it got to do with you?

TRACIE: Yes. Mind your own business.

EMMA: What did you come here for anyway? Nobody wants you –

TARA: Yeah!

LOTTIE: I just - I just - Mummy thought - I wanted - (*Suddenly biting back tears*) Oh you're all too thick to understand!!

She stumbles out of the tent and goes and sits by the side of the stage, her back to the tent, her head down on her knees.

TARA: Charming!

She yawns and stretches.

EMMA: Snobby cat!

Sophie snuffles.

TARA: Sophie shut up, or I'll smother you!

They all settle down to rest again, Sophie desperately trying to muffle her sobs.

The attention shifts to the other tent. Helen sits up suddenly.

HELEN: What's that disgusting smell?

There is a slight pause. Anne, who has been surreptitiously rubbing some lotion into her legs, sits up and looks at Helen.

ANNE: It's my insect lotion. I've been bitten all over. This puts them off.

POLLY: I'm not surprised. That'd put anything off. Smells like cats' pee and cabbage water.

ANNE: It's very effective. No insect can stand it.

JOANNE: Neither can any human beings. Ugh! It stinks!

DEBBIE: Yeah. What do you want to put it on now for?

ANNE: I've got a very sensitive skin. I get bitten easy, then I come out in great big bumps.

HELEN: (*Holding up the bottle*) Is this it?

ANNE: Yes. The Chemist recommended it.

HELEN: (*Pretending to read*) To be used with care. Contains – disinfectant, bad eggs, doggy poo, mouldy cauliflower and essence of nappy water. Fatal at five yards to all insects, animals and humans.

ANNE: Oh shut up! Give it back.

HELEN: You're not putting any more of this stuff on! We'll all be gassed!

> *Helen suddenly lunges forward towards the tent flap and flings the bottle out of the tent. It skims along the ground and lands a few feet away from Lottie, who glances towards it, decides it is another insult and hunches her shoulders and turns away.*

ANNE: I hate you, Helen Leigh!

> *She crawls out of the tent and wanders around looking for the bottle. Lottie ignores her.*

ANNE: What's the matter with you?

LOTTIE: Nothing.

ANNE: What you doing out here?

LOTTIE: Sitting.

ANNE: (*Sarcastically*) No! Really!

LOTTIE: (*Muttering*) Came out for some air. (*Pause*) What do you want? You're supposed to be resting.

ANNE: That Helen Leigh chucked my insect lotion out. I hate her!

LOTTIE: That's it. Over there.

> *She gestures towards the bottle. Anne picks it up and stands looking at Lottie.*

ANNE: Lucky it didn't break. She'd have paid for it if it had.

> *There is no reply from Lottie.*

ANNE: Are you crying?

LOTTIE: No. I'm not.

ANNE: Yes you are.

LOTTIE: Well... They're horrible in my tent.

ANNE: Yes. They're horrible in mine as well. Just because I've got a sensitive skin. (*Thrusting her arm under Lottie's nose*) Look. There! Do you reckon that's a bad smell?

LOTTIE: (*Drawing back. Doubtfully*) No. It's - all right. Smells a bit like the stuff you put down the lavatory.

ANNE: Well, it's very good. It kills insects. Do you want some?

LOTTIE: Er. Thank you.

ANNE: (*Handing her the bottle*) Apply liberally. All exposed areas of the skin.

Lottie dabs a very little on her arm.

LOTTIE: Thank you.

There is a slight pause.

ANNE: Do you like it here?

LOTTIE: Not much.

ANNE: What did you come for?

LOTTIE: Well... Mummy thought it would do me good. She and Daddy have gone to Juan-les-Pins - that's in the South of France - and Jeremy – that's my brother – he's just got engaged and he's gone to stay with Victoria's family -

ANNE: Are you the youngest?

LOTTIE: There's only me and Jeremy. He's ten years older than me. I was a mistake.

ANNE: I reckon we were all mistakes in our family. All six of us. Half the time I don't reckon my Mum knows which is which.

LOTTIE: Why did you come here?

ANNE: Get away from 'em all! I'm the oldest. I have to look after 'em while me Mum's at work.

LOTTIE: (*Delicately*) Is that why you're always late for school?

ANNE: Yeah. Takes me ages. Me Mum goes out at five o'clock - she's got a cleaning job up town - and I have to get the twins to Mrs Allen - she's the Minder - Louise and Gemma to Nursery, and Paul goes to St. Joseph's. Janice fixed for me to come here. To get a break. Not much of a rest though, is it? All this 'Do this, do that! At the double! Jump to it!' Like being in the Army.

LOTTIE: Supposed to be good for us.

ANNE: I thought we'd be sleeping in the House. Have you noticed Janice is keeping her head down? She knows it's a dead loss here. Waste of money, I reckon.

LOTTIE: (*Very surprised*) Oh! (*Pause*) Are you paying then?

ANNE: (*After a slight pause. Defiantly*) Yes. Why?

LOTTIE: Oh. Nothing. I just thought...

ANNE: (*Aggressively*) What?

LOTTIE: I just - happened to know that some people - got a bit of help - other people paid - well, that the money came out of a special fund -

ANNE: Oh yes?

LOTTIE: Yes...

> *There is an embarrassed pause. Lottie tries to retrieve the situation.*

(*Hastily*) I think it's a good thing. So that everybody can have a holiday. And they don't say at all - who's paid the full amount - like me - and who's had to be helped from the Fund. I think that's marvellous. We're all the same then. At my First School some of us took cheques for our School Dinners. For the whole term. And then, of course, we didn't give any dinner money in each week. So you couldn't tell the difference between the well-off kids and those on free dinners. So nobody got embarrassed. I think that's good, don't you?

ANNE: (*Stung*) Yes. You would think that. I bet you told everybody, though, didn't you? Of course you weren't on free dinners. Well, I don't need no charity. Me and my Mum we pay on the nail - for everything. Not like your sort. Get everything on tick for months and months. 'Oh Goodness! Haven't I paid you for five months? Naughty me! How much is that? £500? Let me give you a cheque...' My uncle's got a greengrocer's. He knows your sort.

LOTTIE: There's no need to get worked up. I wasn't meaning you -

ANNE: Give me that lotion. I hope you get bit! All over.

She snatches her bottle of lotion away from Lottie, goes back into the tent and flings herself, face down, onto her bed. Lottie stands up and looks after her for a moment, biting her lip. She glances towards her own tent. Then suddenly she rushes off downstage right. Joanne sits up and sniffs as Anne re-enters the tent.

JOANNE: That's better! It does wear off in the fresh air then, that stink?

ANNE: (*Head down, motionless*) Yes.

DEBBIE: Oh Gawd!! What's the matter now? You gonna sulk all day?

Anne sits up, throwing her lotion down angrily.

ANNE: No. It's not that. It's that Lottie.

POLLY: Oh. Ignore her. I always do.

HELEN: I suppose she has her insect lotion specially made up by the Queen's insect man!

ANNE: No. She was just going on about people who were being paid for - by the fund...

POLLY: We all are, aren't we?

HELEN: I am!

DEBBIE: So'm I! you don't want to take any notice of that. Her Mum and Dad gave a stack of money to the Club. She's only showing off.

JOANNE: Wouldn't use our own money to come to this dump!

From the other tent Tara gives three piercing whistles.

HELEN: Sh! That's the other tent. That means Janice and Hitler are about. Quiet everybody!

She gives three whistles in return and the two tents settle down in near silence - though not without a certain amount of stifled giggling.

Silence. Kate and Rosie return to their respective tents. Rosie downstage left and Kate downstage right.

ROSIE: What you all so quiet for?

HELEN: We thought you were Janice.

JOANNE: Or Hitler.

ROSIE: No. that's the good bit. Hitler's been stung on the eyelid by a great big wasp and his eye's all swelled up. Janice's driving him to the Doctor's. And Mrs Hicks is over in the boys' field. So there's nobody about. Janice says we're to be sensible till she gets back.

They fall about with laughter at the thought.

DEBBIE: I wish I'd been there. Bit of excitement. Supposed to be an adventure holiday. Some adventure. We haven't done nothing at all!

POLLY: We've only been here a day. And you don't usually get adventures on a Sunday.

JOANNE: Janice says there's a lot planned -

ROSIE: Listen. That's the thing. You can get up now. Me and Kate've been up to the House. And we've had an idea.

HELEN: What?

ROSIE: No. Outside. With the others. Come on. Quick!

The girls crawl out from both tents and gather centre stage, stretching and crowding round Kate and Rosie to hear what they have to say.

TARA: Oh that's better. If we have to have a rest like little kids every day I'm going home.

TRACIE: I bet they'll make us write post-cards -

KATE: Shut up and listen! Me and Rosie have been up to the House. It's smashing! There's dormitories with proper beds, and big staircases and banisters and little hidey-holes and everything. Lot better than this rotten old field!

ROSIE: Now. We're all agreed that we want to get put in the House. Yes?

EMMA: But that's only if it rains.

KATE: Or if we can't use the tents.

TARA: What do you mean?

ROSIE: If the tents were ruined.

HELEN: What?

KATE: Flooded.

DEBBIE: How could they be? It hasn't rained for weeks.

KATE: That tap - over there. Where we get the washing-up and drinking water.

ROSIE: There's a long pipe - in the yard. Connects it up to a tap outside the kitchen window.

ANNE: Well?

KATE: This field slopes, doesn't it?

ROSIE: If we turn the tap full on in the yard –

KATE: They use that tap for washing the yard down. It don't half give a jet of water. I went to get a drink and it nearly knocked my head off -

ROSIE: Then we turn this tap on and forget to turn it off...

KATE: And go for a long walk....

ROSIE: By the time Janice and Hitler get back from the Doctor's and we come back from our walk...

KATE: The water'll pour down the slope, into the tents and soak everything through!

SOPHIE: I don't want my things all soaked.

KATE: Well, put anything you don't want to get wet off the ground.

ROSIE: Just leave your bed on the floor.

KATE: And a few clothes.

TARA: Will it run into the tents? Won't it just soak in and go all muddy?

KATE: There's nowhere else for it to go. It's got to run down the slope and the ground's as hard as iron. It can't soak in.

JOANNE: They'll know it's us.

ROSIE: Not if we're not here. If we stay out long enough -

KATE: We can watch from the woods down there till somebody gets back.

TRACIE: Yeah. We could say it definitely wasn't on when we left and somebody must have turned it on while we was away!

POLLY: Yeah. They couldn't prove anything.

There is a moment's thoughtful pause while they digest the idea.

ANNE: (*Meaningfully*) Good job Lottie's not here. She'd only tell.

TARA: Where's she got to?

KATE: (*Delighted*) Yeah. That's the other good bit. We saw Lottie - me and Rosie - from the bedroom window. Walking off down the road!

ROSIE: Away from here. Towards the village.

There is a pause.

HELEN: What do you reckon she's up to?

KATE: I dunno.

ROSIE: Running away, I suppose.

ANNE: Good job too!

POLLY: (*Slowly*) Shouldn't we go after her?

TARA: What for? If she wants to muck about, let her!

SOPHIE: Good riddance!

POLLY: But she doesn't know her way round or anything...

ANNE: That's her own stupid fault isn't it?

EMMA: She can always call a cab!

The others, except for Polly and Helen, giggle.

HELEN: She might get abducted.

POLLY: Or raped, or something!

TRACIE: She shouldn't try to show off.

JOANNE: She's the one that keeps telling us what to do.

DEBBIE: Yeah. I'm not trailing off after her. In this heat.

KATE: (*Slowly*) And if she's not here when we come back... They'll think *she* left the tap on.

> *There is a moment's silence.*

POLLY: (*Hesitantly*) I think that's a bit mean. Letting them blame her -

ANNE: Why not ? She's paid for it!!!

> *They shriek and giggle at this, except for Helen and Polly. Kate runs up and turns on the tap. There is an immediate sound effect of running water. They all rush off. Polly and Helen decide there is nothing they can do, and run off after the others. The lights begin to fade. The sound of the water splashing onto hard ground becomes louder and louder as it cascades down the slope towards the tents.*

THE END

THE CHILDREN'S WARD

CHARACTERS

PATRICK

CHRIS

MARCUS

VALERIE

KEITH

The play is set in the children's ward of a large modern hospital in the 1990s.

THE CHILDREN'S WARD

*A six-bedded ward in a bright modern hospital. It is a children's ward. There are three beds on each side. Each bed has a locker beside it, and one or two plastic chairs. There is a door, left, to the playroom, and another, right, to the corridor, the offices, etc. The windows have cards, cut-outs, and brightly coloured pictures and posters pasted up on them, including one of **Postman Pat**. The window-sill is full of cards and books. Five beds are empty. The bed nearest to the window has been transformed into a small 'living area.' There are cartons of juice, packets of biscuits, crisps, mousse and yoghurt cartons and coke bottles on the locker, together with a Sony Walkman, some comics and a few books. Carefully placed on a wooden drawing board on the bed is an intricate cardboard model of an Elizabethan house. On the window-sill, in the corner beside the bed, are several other models - all beautifully made. The house on the bed is unfinished. A cardboard shoebox of pens, glue, etc. stands beside it.*

The bed next to it is bare by comparison. A simple cardboard sign saying 'Nothing by mouth' hangs over the bed. The locker has a jug and glass on it. A tall, pale-faced boy is lying, in dressing gown and pyjamas, on the bed, staring into space. Patrick - aged thirteen - has the air of someone passing through. But he looks worried, even a little frightened.

The bed diagonally opposite him has been carefully made, the sheets tightly tucked in. There is a pile of books on the locker. The window-sill beside the bed is full of brightly coloured 'get well soon' cards. The other four beds in the ward have obviously been recently vacated, the bedclothes tumbled, comics, books, toys lying higgledy-piggledy all over them.

Patrick gets up and crosses to the bed with the 'get well' cards. He picks up one of the cards and stands reading it.

> *Chris enters quietly and sees Patrick with the card. Chris is a delicate-looking boy with a permanently 'closed in' expression on his face, a suggestion of long term pain. He is fifteen. He walks with a pronounced limp.*

CHRIS: That's Darren. They took him this morning. He's having a big heart operation.

> *Patrick, embarrassed, puts the card back carefully and scoots back to his bed and sits down rather self-consciously.*

PATRICK: Oh. I was just looking...

CHRIS: He's been here ages. His heart's pretty well rubbish. He keeps going blue.

PATRICK: Oh.

> *Chris limps back to his bed, sits down and looks speculatively at Patrick.*

CHRIS: When did you get in?

PATRICK: (*A touch of pride*) Half past four this morning. They thought I had a burst appendix. (*Lamely*) But it's gone off a bit.

CHRIS: I didn't hear you.

PATRICK: No. You were all asleep. The boy in that corner bed shouted out something. Well, sort of screamed. I didn't hear what he said. I'd been in Emergency - or whatever it is - since one o' clock. Then they brought me here. They just ignored him...

CHRIS: Wayne. Yeah they would. He's a real nuisance. He's always shouting in his sleep. They ought to move him. Keeping everybody awake, They take your appendix out?

PATRICK: No. I don't know whether they're going to. They're going to do some tests. But I don't think that's for appendix...

CHRIS: That, my son, is all you get in here. Tests. Tests. Tests. Never bother to tell you what for. Nothing by mouth for twelve hours. No liquids, no solids, no nothing. Needles up your bum. Tubes down your throat... Then just when you think you're gonna get a bit of peace they whip you down to the theatre, cut you open, have a rummage round inside, then sew you up again and send you back up here. You don't feel like eating for a week after that.

PATRICK: (*Looking worried*) Oh... Are you here for - have you got something the matter with your leg?

CHRIS: No. I've just broke a bone in my ankle. I did that in here. I've got a liver disease.

He is very dismissive as if he does not wish to discuss this.

I broke this skateboarding down the corridor.

PATRICK: (*Amazed and quite impressed*) Is that allowed?

CHRIS: No.

He settles himself on his bed and begins to work on his model. There is a silence. Patrick watches him. Chris examines one piece of the model, sets it down, and looks round angrily.

CHRIS: Have you been mucking about with this?

PATRICK: No. I haven't touched it. Honest. I wouldn't.

CHRIS: (*Unconvinced*) Hmmmm. (*He carries on working*) Only this isn't just mucking about... This is complicated work. It's not a toy. I shall have a whole village when I've finished. I've got the Church and the pub and a row of cottages done already. This is the Manor House.

PATRICK: It's very good. I'm useless at that sort of thing.

CHRIS: You need practice... But it's not a toy. My stupid Auntie Kath came in last Sunday. 'Oh! Aren't you a clever boy! Isn't that fiddly? I think it's a good idea to have something to play with in here. Gives you an interest.' Then she sat down on a whole dry-stone wall I'd got drying on a chair. Stuck to her stupid frock. She didn't bother to offer me a word of apology mind! Just moaned about the glue on her skirt. Kept on and on. 'Does it show? Has it marked it? I'm going on from here you know! I've got a function this evening at The Bull at Richmond.' Silly cow! Do you know what she brought me? Action Man and his Jungle Campaign! I told her, 'Auntie Kath, I am sixteen next birthday.' My Dad told me not to be so lippy or he'd fetch me one. I love visiting! At least I've been here so long they only come once a week. It was murder at first. Every day! How long are you here for?

PATRICK: Just a couple of days I think.

CHRIS: Kid with kidney failure had that bed last.

He looks suspiciously at his model.

Somebody's been messing about with this. Look. This is all bent back. Shouldn't be like that.

PATRICK: There was a little kid running round in here earlier. Come to visit that boy with the glasses. I didn't take much notice of him. I was - I was - (*Selecting his words carefully*) They'd just brought me back - I was - reading. He was playing with a little car. His Mum took him to the Playroom.

CHRIS: Oh... Dominic! Marcus's brother. He's a real pest. Came up to me last week and grabbed hold of that box I keep all the Pentels and glue and stuff in. I told him to bring it back. He wouldn't. So I took it. He screamed the place down. His Mum just sat there. Then she turned on me! 'Oh, couldn't he just play with them for a while? He likes the colours. He loves drawing.' So I told her it wasn't a toy and they were mine. She just said, 'Oh he won't hurt anything. I'll see you get them back.' Then she let him chuck them all over the floor.

PATRICK: What did you do?

CHRIS: Well, I picked them all up and took them away. I said I needed them. He screamed blue murder and Sister came in and his Mum said, 'He just wants to borrow the crayons for a minute but I'm afraid we're being a bit dog-in-the-manger!'

PATRICK: Oh.

CHRIS: Sister was great. She just said, 'Christopher has been making his models for a long time, and there's a Stanley knife in that box. I don't think it's a very suitable toy for a small child, There's lots of toys in the Playroom.'

PATRICK: She seems nice. The Sister...

CHRIS: Yeah. She's all right. They're all all right.

He becomes absorbed in his model and suddenly seems to have no further interest in Patrick, who watches him a little apprehensively.

PATRICK: Er -

He stops. Chris is taking no notice of him at all.

CHRIS: Mmmm?

PATRICK: Nothing.

He picks up a book and attempts to read it. But he is not really seeing the words on the page.

Marcus comes in. He is lively, energetic, bright, a long-stay patient. He is much more middle-class than his accent (which he adopts to be one of the crowd) would suggest. He looks at Patrick and decides to ignore him for the moment.

MARCUS: 'Lo Chris.

He goes and sits on his bed which is opposite Patrick's.

CHRIS: Hello.

He carries on with his model.

MARCUS: Where's Keith?

CHRIS: Dunno. (*Looking up suddenly*) Your little brother's here. He's in the Playroom.

MARCUS: I know. That's why I came in here. He's screaming the place down. He wants the little house, he says. My Mum keeps shovelling him into the Wendy House and he keeps kicking the other kids. I wish she wouldn't keep bringing him.

CHRIS: (*Quite detached, concentrating on his model*) It must be embarrassing having a brother like that.

MARCUS: My Mum spoils him rotten. I tell her not to bring him but she thinks he might get what I've got so she wants him to get used to hospital.

He gets up and crosses to Chris's bed, staring openly at Patrick.

CHRIS: He's been mucking about with my models again. Your Mum's got no control over him.

MARCUS: I know. (*To Patrick, flatly*) What's your name?

PATRICK: Patrick.

MARCUS: What's the matter with you?

PATRICK: (*Putting his book down and swinging his legs down onto the floor*) Suspected appendicitis. I've got to have some tests though. Would you like to sit down?

MARCUS: No thanks.

He moves nearer to Chris's bed. A young nurse, Valerie, appears in the doorway. She is friendly and easy-going, but very junior - scarcely older than the boys.

VALERIE: Oh there you are, Marcus! What are you doing here? Your Mum and your little brother are in the Playroom. (*Knowing exactly what he is up to*) What are you up to, running off when they've come all this way to see you?

MARCUS: (*Sidling towards the door furthest from the playroom*) I was just going to the toilet. I won't be a minute.

He darts off before Valerie can say anything else to him.

CHRIS: (*Amused*) You're wasting your time. He hates his brother. Mind you I don't blame him. If that horrible little -

VALERIE: (*Warning*) Chris! Language!

CHRIS: What did I say?

VALERIE: Ah! It's what you were going to say though, isn't it? Can't have you using bad language in front of our new patient, can we?

She smiles sunnily at Patrick who has, however, wandered off into a world of his own.

CHRIS: I was only going to say that if that little darling touches my models again I'll rearrange his face for him.

Valerie has noticed Patrick's abstracted, worried air and crosses and sits on the end of his bed.

VALERIE: Come on now! Let's have some sort of smile! You look as if you'd lost a fiver and found 5p! You've still got your appendix haven't you?

PATRICK: (*With an attempt at a grin*) Yeah!

VALERIE: Well then! We're not going to eat you!

PATRICK: That's another thing. When can *I* eat ? I'm starving!

VALERIE: Not just yet. When the Doctor's been.

CHRIS: That's what they're like here. First three days they don't let you have any food. It's the Government cuts. Then, if they don't reckon your chances are too good they don't bother to feed you at all - saves money on the catering.

VALERIE: (*Laughing*) That'll do, Chris!

CHRIS: You've got to be fighting fit to keep the food down they give you here, anyway. God! I don't know where they get it from. I'm going to use some of the fish fingers to do the thatched roofs on my cottages... Paint 'em black and put dots on 'em you could play dominoes with 'em!

> *Valerie and Patrick give a slight laugh. Chris cuts out a further section of his model. There is a slight pause.*

CHRIS: (*Casually*) How's Darren?

VALERIE: (*Carefully*) I don't know. He's still in the Theatre.

> *Silence. Keith comes in. He is a sullen, suspicious boy who does not grasp things very quickly and suspects people are trying to make fun of him. He goes straight to his bed which is in the corner, next to Marcus's bed.*

VALERIE: Hello, Keith. What've you been up to?

KEITH: (*Aggressively*) Watching the telly. Trying to. Can't you tell Marcus's Mum to go home with that kid? He kept running in and changing the channel and screaming.

VALERIE: (*Wearily*) Oh dear...

KEITH: He's been here since this morning. I don't think they should let people come visiting you in hospital being a nuisance.

CHRIS: What you worried about? Your Mum hasn't been since Christmas!

KEITH: I don't want her to come, do I? Being a nuisance to everybody.

VALERIE (*Hastily*) Is Marcus in the playroom?

KEITH: No. Nor his Mum. Just his brother. That little black kid from the baby ward scratched his face, 'cos he took his lorry off him. He didn't half yell. And he kicked him.

VALERIE: (*Getting up from the end of Patrick's bed*) Oh dear! No rest for the wicked! Roll on tea-time. Tracy'll be on again then.

> *She begins to go out of the door to the playroom.*

CHRIS: You can bring me my tea at four o' clock. I'm feeling a bit low. I need looking after. I'll have cucumber sandwiches, and tea with lemon, and strawberries and cream please.

VALERIE: Private patient are we? You'll get bread and marge and plum jam and a bit of angel cake if you're lucky!

She goes out, back to the playroom. Keith, making sure that no-one can see what he's doing, takes a chocolate bar from his locker and lies down on his bed with his back to the rest of them.

CHRIS: They do the teas in the Playroom. You can load up and bring it back here if you want 'cos there's always masses of little kids chucking jam about. I always bring mine back here. Not that it's worth eating. I've got a load of my own stuff in my locker. Do you want a bit of Twix?

PATRICK: I'm not allowed yet. Thanks.

CHRIS: Oh no better not, then. They might trace it back to me. Take a bar of Twix out in that playroom and you've had it. They swarm all over you - smelly nappies and all. I can't stand little kids.

PATRICK: I wouldn't mind something to eat. I'm starving. I haven't had anything at all since six o'clock yesterday. That's over twenty hours! When do the doctors came round?

CHRIS: About three usually. This glue's rubbish.

He gets up irritably, limps across to the window and stares disgustedly at the vividly-coloured poster taped up on the window.

CHRIS: I am sick and tired of Postman bleedin' Pat.

He takes a Pentel and draws a large curly moustache on the poster.

PATRICK: How long are you staying? I mean - when are you going out? Have you got to have an operation?

CHRIS: (*Briefly*) 'Spect so. I dunno. They keep changing their minds.

PATRICK: (*Carefully*) I expect you get a bit bored.

CHRIS: You can say that again. (*Gesturing towards his model*) I never had any time for this sort of thing before I came in here. Just shows what hospital does to you. I've spent hours on it... When I do go home my Mum'll shove it all in a carrier bag and crumple it all up. Then after a bit she'll put it out for the dustman. 'Oh Christopher we can't have that cluttering the place up - collecting dust!'

PATRICK: Won't she let you set it up it in your room?

CHRIS: (*Jeering*) My room! My cupboard you mean. Get the bed in my room and you can't shut the door. I have to stand on the window sill to get dressed - I'll get arrested one of these days. I suppose you've got a lovely big room with a train set and a snooker table and your own telly.

PATRICK: (*Quickly*) No - (*Muttering*) It's not that big.

CHRIS: I bet!... At least there's a bit of space in here... I was in the Men's Ward for a couple of weeks before Christmas. That was terrible. All these old men coughing and spitting! There was one bloke in the bed next to me, he'd had gallstones - and he'd got them in a jam-jar on his locker. Disgusting! Just like little pebbles they were, and he kept showing them to everybody. Then there was this bloke in the corner bed kept smoking his pipe under the covers when nobody was around. I reckon it was shredded underpants he was smoking - Phew!! It was murder.

PATRICK: Is that why you came back here?

CHRIS: No. They decided it was bad for me to be there. They kept snuffing it, you see, in the Old Men's Ward. You know, you wake up in the morning and there's another set of curtains drawn -

PATRICK: (*Shuddering*) Oh that's horrible. Do they leave the bodies behind the curtains?

CHRIS: Nah! Take 'em out on trolleys when nobody's looking. The last night I was in there I was fast asleep, and this old guy - ever so little he was - and he came over to my bed and got hold of my wrist and shook me and he kept saying, 'I'm going... I'm going!' Scared the life out of me, I can tell you.

PATRICK: What did you do?

CHRIS: I said, 'Well go on then!' and shoved him on the floor. Then I screamed blue murder for the night nurse... He was another curtain case by the morning.

PATRICK: I couldn't stand that.

CHRIS: It's 'cos I was fifteen. They thought I was too old for this ward, but after that, they decided I'd get psychologically disturbed if I stayed there so I came back here. Valerie - that nurse that was here just now - she says they ought to have teenage wards. They did where she comes from.

PATRICK: Where's that?

CHRIS: Oh some dump up North. Peterborough or somewhere. Near Birmingham anyway.

Marcus returns, peering round the door cautiously to make sure that the coast is clear.

MARCUS: Has she gone?

CHRIS: Valerie? Yes.

MARCUS: Good.

He comes into the ward and crosses and sits on the end of his bed and looks cheerfully at Chris and Patrick.

CHRIS: She'll be back though... She's madly in love with me.

As he speaks he is reading the instructions on his model and his mind is on that

She can't keep away from me... I have this problem with all the nurses... (*He looks across at Marcus*) Anyway she'll be looking for you. Leroy's scratched your brother's face open.

MARCUS: (*Unimpressed*) Oh, he does that to everybody... Mind you, it's a brilliant idea when it comes to my brother. There's some horrible kids in this place but he's worse than any of them. My Mum doesn't believe in violence so she never hits him - she goes berserk when I do. And she sits up all night with my Dad discussing my aggressive tendencies and where she's gone wrong.

He chuckles delightedly.

CHRIS: Your Mum's a nutcase.

MARCUS: (*Sighing*) Yes, I know. She goes to consciousness raising groups... She's going veggie as well. She cooks these great big panfuls of beans and stuff. Looks like puke. She reckons it's diet why I'm in here. My Dad stops off at McDonalds on the way home from work and says he's not too hungry when he gets in. So she saves up all the bean stuff and puts some lentils in it and gives it him the next day. Do you know, she won't let me and my brother have any aggressive toys or anything. She's trying to find a Save the Whale game for my computer. I can't have nasty War games 'cos she's trying to breed a better sort of boy... My brother's the most violent little devil ever. I hate him. He got chucked out of his playgroup last week.

PATRICK: What for?

MARCUS: He set fire to the Wendy House.

They laugh. Keith turns over angrily to face them.

KEITH: I wish you'd shut up. I'm trying to get to sleep.

MARCUS: That's all you ever do. It's half past two in the afternoon, you know, not midnight.

KEITH: Well, I get tired. When they bringing Darren back?

CHRIS: Dunno.

MARCUS: They were all rushing about with bottles of blood when I was down the corridor. But I couldn't see anything.

KEITH: You're not supposed to go down there. Sister'll murder you!

MARCUS: I crawled past the office on hands and knees. She didn't see me. Nobody saw me. I hid in that little alcove by the lifts to Casualty. I had a look in. There's nobody there much today.

KEITH: I've been to Casualty.

MARCUS: What for?

KEITH: I stuck a wax crayon up my nose and I couldn't get it out.

Marcus roars with laughter.

CHRIS: When was this? Last week?

KEITH: No! I was in the Infants!

MARCUS: I thought you still were.

KEITH: It was awful. They pushed these long steel things up my nose and twisted them round. It took four nurses to hold me down.

MARCUS: What did you do a stupid thing like that for?

KEITH: I don't know. It was a green crayon. Viknesh wanted it. So I just stuck it up my nose and it broke off and got stuck.

MARCUS: They should have shoved a wick up your nose and set light to it and then all the wax would have melted and dripped out.

KEITH: (*Puzzled*) No. They couldn't do that. It would be too hot.

MARCUS: (*Jeering*) No -o-o-o! Oh go back to sleep.

Valerie returns, looking distressed and unwilling to talk. Marcus sidles across to the door, ready to disappear.

CHRIS: There he goes! Stop him! What's the little monster done now?

VALERIE: What? Oh... No. I haven't come for Marcus. Your brother's all right, I think... I've just...Sister's sent me to collect these...

She crosses to Darren's bed and collects up his 'get well' cards. Marcus stands stock-still in the doorway; Keith watches her puzzledly; Patrick, with dawning realization. He opens his mouth as if to speak, thinks better of it and picks up his book and stares unseeingly at it. It is as if the shutters have come down on Chris. Blank-faced, he goes to his bed and picks up his model, apparently absorbed in it.

KEITH: What are you taking them for?

VALERIE: (*Carefully*) Darren's Mum will be here - er - later. I'm just tidying up. Sister wants these in the office...

She stops. There is a tense pause.

CHRIS: How is Darren?

He does not look up from his model. He drops the words delicately, like pebbles into a pool. The only possible emotion he expresses is a kind of repressed anger. Valerie bites her lip. She is too inexperienced to handle this situation very successfully.

VALERIE: Oh. He's - fine. It's just he's being taken elsewhere. (*Hurriedly*) Sister will be along in a minute. She can tell you all about it. I've got to go and see to the little ones' teas...

She goes out, left, towards the playroom, glad to escape. The four boys are quite still.

KEITH: What's she mean, elsewhere? Why's she taken his cards away? Marcus!

Slowly, Marcus crosses and sits on the end of Darren's bed. Keith takes a step towards him.

KEITH: Marcus. What does she mean? What's happened to Darren? Why are they taking him somewhere else?

Chris puts aside his model and limps angrily across to Keith.

CHRIS: *(In a ferocious undertone)* Shut up, shut your stupid fat face!! Go back to bed and stop driving everybody spare! I'm sick of your stupid voice, moaning on. Do you hear me, you stupid git!

Patrick watches anxiously, Marcus lowers his head. Keith sits down abruptly. Chris limps back to his own bed, and sits down becoming absorbed, apparently, in his model.

KEITH: *(Whining)* What have I done? What did I say? You've got no right to talk to me like that, Christopher Greenway. You're not the boss of this ward.

But no-one is paying him any attention. He lies down on his bed with his back to them all, hunched up and angry. The others are all silent and still.

CHRIS: *(Singing tunelessly under his breath)* Postman Pat – Postman Pat - Postman Pat and his black and white cat… '

The four boys are all quite still as the lights fade.

THE END

THE PRESS GANG

CHARACTERS

SUZI

SIMON

TIM

MANDY

GEMMA

KEVIN

ANTHONY

CHARLOTTE

JULIE

ANGELA

The play is set in the Reprographics Room of a large modern school in the 1990s.

THE PRESS GANG

A large, ill-lit classroom overlooking an outside alleyway between buildings. All that is visible outside is another wall, with windows onto more classrooms. The room has been set up as a print-room with printers, copiers, computers, piles of paper and photographic equipment ranged around. A large pin-board is on one wall where various posters, programmes and magazine covers, are displayed together with posters advertising photographic exhibitions and courses etc. There are piles of papers, marking pens, paste, Sellotape and scissors on the table.

Suzi is sitting on the floor in front of the table. Her legs drawn up, her arms clasped round her knees, her head down, staring broodingly into space. She is not visible from the door. It is late afternoon and what little light that gets into the room is fading. The place has a secret, hidden-away feel to it. The door opens suddenly and Simon rushes in. He shouts back over his shoulder to someone outside.

SIMON: I must have left it in here. You go on and get the table.

Whistling cheerfully, he begins to hunt around the room. Suzi stays very still as if by doing so she will not be seen by him. Simon, still searching for his bag, comes downstage of the table and sees her. He stops and looks rather guiltily at her. She is aware of him but does not look at him.

What are you doing on the floor?

SUZI: Sitting. (*Pause*) What does it look like?

There is another pause. Simon tries to speak casually.

SIMON: (*Awkwardly*) I've left my bag somewhere. If it's not here I don't know where it is. You haven't seen it have you?

SUZI: No.

SIMON: Me and Peter were going to have a game of table tennis. Before the meeting. (*Silence*) I was going to come. Honest. (*As Suzi does not speak*) Have you been here since?... You haven't just stopped here? Haven't you been home?

SUZI: S'got nothing to do with you.

Pause. Simon really wants to go but feels he can't.

SIMON: You don't want to sit there like that. Can't see you from the door. You could get locked in. Overnight.

Suzi looks at him contemptuously.

SUZI: (*Sarcastically*) There's a meeting here in ten minutes. You're coming to it. Remember? If you can spare the time from your table tennis.

SIMON: No. I hadn't forgotten. There's no need to be like that! Do you reckon anybody else'll bother to come after the way you went on at lunch-time?

SUZI: I did not go on.

SIMON: Yes you did. You've got a rotten temper. And people wouldn't take that sort of thing from Miss Harper, let alone you. It's not just your magazine you know.

SUZI: Don't keep saying that!! Just because you'd rather muck about at meetings and leave all the work to everybody else -

SIMON: Look. Just calm down. If you keep on like that people will just give up. Too much hassle.

Suzi looks mulishly at him for a moment then turns away.

SUZI: Your bag's over there. Under the chair.

Simon crosses and collects his bag from under the chair where it has been pushed. He turns back to Suzi.

SIMON: You haven't been home have you?

SUZI: Mind your own business.

SIMON: Was it - was it Mandy?... She didn't mean it –

SUZI: How do you know?

SIMON: Well - she can be really horrible if she likes but I don't think she meant what she said -

SUZI: What did you all laugh for then? (*Triumphantly, as he does not answer*) You're a real hypocrite, Simon. You join in when - Mandy and the others - then you come and crawl to me when there's nobody about!

SIMON: I didn't join in.

SUZI: You laughed.

SIMON: No I didn't. I didn't actually say anything, in fact. If you weren't so busy bossing everybody about you might notice. Anyway, don't you know when people are joking?

SUZI: Mandy wasn't joking.

SIMON: Yes she was. Well half and half anyway. She's like that with everybody.

SUZI: Oh yeah?

SIMON: Everybody got a bit fed up. It was just the heat of the moment.

SUZI: If it was just the heat of the moment it must have been a long moment for her to write all this.

She seizes a piece of A4 paper, covered on both sides with flamboyant handwriting, from the table and thrusts it at him.

Just a little joke! What was she going to do with this? Print two hundred copies and sell it to everybody I suppose.

Simon reads the paper through.

Nice little joke isn't it? I thought it was a big laugh when I read it.

She goes towards the door.

SIMON: Where are you going?

SUZI: The toilet. You'd better go and play table tennis. Pete'll wonder where you are.

She goes out. Simon stands looking at the paper. He folds it and puts it in his pocket, as Tim rushes in, carrying a camera and a pile of photographs.

TIM: (*Cheerfully*) Hello, Simon. Where is everybody?

SIMON: It's only ten to.

TIM: Look. What do you think of these?

He prepares to spread out his photographs on the table, with great care and considerable satisfaction.

SIMON: (*Hastily*) Not now. Wait till the others get here.

TIM: Yeah. It'd be a shame to waste them on you. I am actually brilliant. There are some pictures there only a genius could have taken.

He examines his camera.

Eight shots left. What's the matter with Suzi?

SIMON: Why?

TIM: Nearly knocked me down in the corridor, then she just screamed 'Oh get out of my way!' She's really boring the way she shouts at everybody.

SIMON: She's got problems.

TIM: (*Mocking him*) Naao! Oh dear. Pore-old-Suzi. Never mind Simon'll kiss it better then.

SIMON: Shut up.

TIM: I just think she's bad-tempered. Gets her knickers in a twist if you ask her what time it is.

Mandy comes in with Gemma.

MANDY: (*With mock surprise*) Oh Madam not here then?

SIMON: Yes. She's gone to the toilet.

GEMMA: I'm not stopping after half past.

MANDY: Nor am I.

No-one takes any notice. Mandy wanders over to the notice-board.

Oh, this place is depressing. Shouldn't we put the chairs round? With a throne for Her Majesty?

Gemma giggles. Simon looks troubled.

SIMON: Oh shut up, Mandy. Leave her alone for five minutes, can't you?

MANDY: You've changed your tune haven't you? Fancy her do you?

SIMON: Don't be stupid. I'm just sick of you two bitching each other all the time. It was you and Suzi started this magazine, wasn't it? I thought you were supposed to be friends.

MANDY: Friends with that! Huh!

Gemma has been riffling through the papers on the table and knocks over a container full of pens, pencils etc.

GEMMA: Whoops!

Simon looks at her, exasperated.

SIMON: And what's she supposed to be here for?

MANDY: She can come if she wants to. It's not your magazine, Simon Dawes.

Tim has been watching them with delight and he now creeps in front of them as they confront one other and crouches, camera at the ready.

TIM: Brilliant. Don't move!

He photographs them. Then stands up and moves away winding on his camera, etc.

That'll look good. With a caption. 'Tempers raised at editorial meeting!'

MANDY: Don't you put that camera down anywhere. Because if you do I'm going to smash it to pieces. I'm sick of you going round taking pictures all the time. Never get a minute's peace.

GEMMA: Yeah. They're horrible pictures as well. Can't tell what they're supposed to be!

TIM: Shows how much you know. I take action shots. I suppose you want to pose. (*Striking a pose and pulling a pouting face*) Wouldn't do you any good. Best way to photograph you is a long shot, out of focus, round a corner

Gemma pulls a face and crosses over to Mandy. They whisper together. Kevin, Anthony and Charlotte come in carrying various papers and folders. Anthony without a word to the others settles himself in the corner and sits absorbedly sketching on a small drawing pad. Kevin sorts through his folder of papers.

KEVIN: Where's Suzi?

SIMON: Toilet. (*Pause*) Look, one of you had better go and fetch her - she's been gone ages.

MANDY: I'm not going.

GEMMA: Nor me.

SIMON: Listen, Gemma, I don't know what you're doing here anyway. Nobody asked you to come. You haven't got a job on the magazine. And I don't think there's a job thick enough for you to do anyway. So don't sit there trying to make trouble or you'll be thrown out.

MANDY: We agreed that anybody who wanted to could come along and help.

SIMON: Yeah. But what's the point if you can't read and write and you can't understand words of more than one syllable! The only job she's fit for is fetching Suzi out of the bog. If she can remember where it is!

GEMMA: I'm not stopping if you talk to me like that!

SIMON: Oh brilliant! She's got the point! She may not have much between the ears, ladies and gentleman, but if you wind her up she goes running off just where you want her to!

GEMMA: You what?

SIMON: It must be exhausting being as thick as you, Gemma. Wouldn't it be easier to understand something once in a while?

CHARLOTTE: Oh shut up, Simon. We can't all be as clever as you!

SIMON: No I know, but you could try a bit harder.

GEMMA: Anyway I *can* read.

> *Kevin looks up with a puzzled expression. He has been working on his papers throughout. He seems a little worried by what he has found there.*

KEVIN: Miss Harper says to get on with things. She'll be a bit late. Can't we start?

> *The door opens suddenly and Suzi comes in. She looks dangerously calm. There is a silence as she enters. She crosses and sits by the table.*

SUZI: Shall we get started then?

MANDY: Ben, Angela and Julie aren't here yet.

CHARLOTTE: I saw Angela and Julie down by the bus-stop. I don't know if they're coming.

KEVIN: Ben's always late.

SUZI: Well, we can't wait for them. We've got a lot to get through. Kevin. Have you done the figures?

MANDY: I thought you and Simon were supposed to be joint editors.

SUZI: Yes. We are. There's no supposed about it.

MANDY: Why are you doing everything then?

SUZI: Because we've got to get on. We'll get through everything quicker if I do it.

MANDY: You reckon you're better than Simon do you?

SUZI: No.

MANDY: You're both the editors. It doesn't mean you're the boss.

TIM: Oh, don't waste time, Mandy. The light's going and I haven't got any flash with me.

MANDY: We're all supposed to be equal. I think we should take a vote. I propose that Simon takes the meeting.

GEMMA: Seconded.

SUZI: She can't do that, She's not even supposed to be here.

MANDY: Yes she is. She's helping me on features.

Simon laughs.

SIMON: Are you sure. She probably thinks features means make-up.

Angela and Julie come in. They are busy talking to each other and do not seem very interested in the meeting.

JULIE: Oh. Am I late? I had to go to the shop.

MANDY: You're just in time. We're having a vote.

CHARLOTTE: It's going to be really boring if every meeting's like this. I've got loads of other things to do.

The others all agree.

ANGELA: What sort of vote?

MANDY: To see who runs this meeting. I propose that Simon does.

JULIE: Oh no. We'll be here all night.

ANGELA: Where's Miss Harper?

KEVIN: Staff meeting. She's going to be late.

Tim and Anthony have wandered upstage and are talking about Anthony's sketches and Tim's photographs.

JULIE: Oh, that's means she won't be here at all! Just when we need her!

ANGELA: What have we got to bother with a vote for?

SIMON: We haven't. I'm not going to take the meeting. So there's no point in voting.

Mandy gives him a venomous look.

MANDY: Well done, Simon!

SUZI: (*In a carefully controlled voice*) Kevin. Would you like to give us your financial report?

CHARLOTTE: Tim! Anthony! Shut up and come here.

They settle down. None of them is really interested in Kevin's report and each carries on with his or her own preoccupations. Charlotte is reading a typescript. Anthony sketches. Tim fiddles with his camera. Suzi stares, unseeingly, ahead. Mandy and Gemma whisper and Angela and Julie play with a walkman. Simon watches Suzi.

KEVIN: There's a bit of a problem about the money. I'm £7.10p short. We sold the complete print run of 250 - well, anyway, we haven't got any left - at 20p a copy that ought to give us £50. Printing costs £25.40p. Loan from Miss Harper to cover materials, films and so on £12.50p. Prize money £5. That adds up to £42.90p. That means I should have £7.10p and I haven't. I don't know where it's gone. That's our profit and we haven't got it.

There is a buzz of conversation.

CHARLOTTE: That's not much! I thought we'd do better than that. It's not worth it is it?

KEVIN: It is the first edition. We've got a lot of stuff for the next one.

We won't need any loans. But we've got to find that £7.10. or we're back where we started.

JULIE: You must have lost it.

CHARLOTTE: Perhaps you gave it to Miss Harper.

ANGELA: Somebody hasn't given in their money for selling the copies.

There is an outraged buzz of chatter. 'I gave all mine in; 'I sold twelve copies'; 'I gave you mine last week'; etc.

SUZI: (*Loudly*) Mandy! (*Pause*) How many did you give away?

MANDY: What do you mean?

SUZI: You gave a whole load of copies away.

MANDY: No I did not.

SUZI: Yes you did.

MANDY: I didn't!!! All right. Prove it then.

CHARLOTTE: You were giving a lot out a break on Tuesday.

There is an uncomfortable pause. They look at Mandy.

MANDY: I might have told a few people they could bring me the money later. (*A buzz of disapproval from the others*) But I didn't give any away!

KEVIN: You're not supposed to do that. We agreed at the last meeting. If people haven't got the money they can't have a copy. You can't run a business like that!

MANDY: Yeah! And who wants to buy this rubbish anyway!

KEVIN: That's not the point. The rest of us managed to sell our copies.

TIM: Yes. I could have sold loads more. People will fight to get hold of my photographs, you know.

ANTHONY: They might fight. They wouldn't pay money though!

KEVIN: Shut up. This is important.

ANTHONY: £7.10p. That's 35 copies not paid for.

TIM: And 10p from somewhere.

MANDY: I only had twenty-five didn't I? So how do you get £7.10p from that? I gave you £5, didn't I?

KEVIN: Yes.

MANDY: So how am I supposed to have given away all these copies?

SIMON: But you just said just now that you did give them away!

ANTHONY: I bought a sketch pad.

KEVIN: How much?

ANTHONY: Can't remember.

KEVIN: Anyway, don't be stupid, you didn't get the money from me. You must have paid for it yourself.

ANTHONY: (*Vaguely*) Oh yes. I think my Mum got it.

KEVIN: Well you'd better give me the receipt but I can't pay you because we haven't got any money.

MANDY: Are we going to go on about this all night - Madam Chairperson?!

KEVIN: We've got to get the money sorted out properly.

ANGELA: All right. You sort it out then and tell us next meeting.

General chorus of assent.

KEVIN: You can't do that!

TIM: We just have!

SUZI: (*Hastily*) Agreed. See to it will you Kevin?

KEVIN: I don't see how.

TIM: You're the treasurer.

KEVIN: It's not fair!

He subsides muttering. Tim pretends to photograph him.

TIM: 'The treasurer sits down to wild applause after giving his report.'

KEVIN: You can shut up!

SUZI: Right. I think we're all agreed that the next edition of the magazine will be on the same lines as the first. It seemed very successful.

CHARLOTTE: I don't know where you're going to get any more articles from.

MANDY: No, nor me.

CHARLOTTE: Nobody wants to write anything for us. I asked Mrs Martindale if she'd make people do something in English and then I could have the best ones.

JULIE: That's not the same though as getting things done for us though is it? I mean it'll be really boring if we just put people's English homework in.

GEMMA: I don't know what you want articles for. They're all boring.

SIMON: What a really great idea! Let's do a magazine Gemma would like. Hundred and forty blank pages for a totally blank mind. Kill two birds with one stone. Save Charlotte the bother of doing any work and give Gemma something she could actually read!

CHARLOTTE: All right then! You try getting people to write anything interesting.

MANDY: I wrote a really interesting article didn't I, Suzi? *(Pause)* Like my interview with Mr Jameson... Only a bit different.

CHARLOTTE: Where is it, then? What's it about?

MANDY: Where is it, Suzi?

There is a tense, unpleasant pause.

SIMON: Probably in the same place as the £7 you - lost.

There is an outbreak of chatter at this.

ANTHONY: I don't think we want all this reading anyway. Why don't we have an edition that's all cartoons? We could have an adventure strip -

SIMON: Because it takes you ages to do one cartoon. We'd all have left by the time you'd finished it.

JULIE: And there's only you interested in adventure strips. I think that's really boring.

SUZI: We've got the letter page and the cookery column -

ANGELA: We haven't got any letters -

SIMON: Make 'em up. That's what they do on real magazines.

ANGELA: You can't do that. Everbody'd know.

JULIE: You might as well. Nobody's going to write to you - 'Angela and the Doc!' Everybody knows you've got more problems than all the rest put together. And you'd tell everybody!

ANGELA: The only problems they'd have is if they'd made your cookery recipe. Broccoli and cheddar pizza! Yeeuch!!!!

They giggle amicably.

SUZI: Look. Please. We've got to get on. What about the competition page? Why isn't Ben here? How are we going to get anything done with everybody being so childish.

Mandy reacts angrily.

Or not turning up. If you say you're going to do something you should stick to it.

TIM: Ben's not coming.

SUZI: Why not?

KEVIN: Because Keith Wilson won the competition.

TIM: Ben gave him the answers.

ANTHONY: They were going to split the prize money.

SUZI: We can't let them do that. It's false pretences.

MANDY: They've done it haven't they? What are you going to do about it?

SUZI: Ben will have to bring the money back.

MANDY: He hasn't got it. Keith Wilson has. And he won't give Ben any.

TIM: Ben's not coming again. He says magazines are boring.

JULIE: Not as boring as his rotten competitions.

GEMMA: No. I couldn't understand them.

SIMON: You couldn't understand **The Teletubbies**.

GEMMA: Shut up!

ANTHONY: We could expose them in the next edition. 'We name the guilty ones!!!' Mandy could do a feature and I could do an identikit picture of them.

TIM: Don't be daft. We know what they look like.

JULIE: Everybody would laugh at us.

ANGELA: They do that anyway.

KEVIN: We could ask Miss Harper -

SUZI: No!!! It's supposed to be our magazine. We're supposed to run it and sort things out for ourselves.

CHARLOTTE: It's too much bother. It was good at first, but it's all hassle now. The money, and writing all the articles, and stopping on after school, and selling them, and everything. Why don't we just stop and - and - oh I dunno - do another one next term... it doesn't have to be a monthly magazine... It's too much trouble -

ANGELA: Yeah. I think that's a good idea. I've got better things to do...

JULIE: And me.

KEVIN: It's not a bad idea. We could make it really good.

MANDY: *(With a triumphant glance at Suzi)* I think it's a brilliant idea. We've had one edition and it was very successful. We don't want to get out another one that's not as good. We can have a meeting next term. Those who are interested. Choose the editor -

SUZI: No!! You can't. We said it was going to be every month. If we stop now we'll never start again. You were all keen. You all wanted to do it. You can't stop now. Tim... Charlotte... Simon... you know - we've got to keep going. Just because we've had a few problems. Everybody says how good the magazine is. We've got to go on. It's important -

MANDY: Yeah! For you. It's all down to you isn't it? '**Suzi's Weekly** edited by Suzi, with in-depth interviews by Suzi. Turn to page five for a full page picture of Suzi... On page ten, Suzi tells us what it's like to be Suzi... Back page, a day in the life of our Busy Editor, Suzi... All you ever wanted to know about Suzi! ...' I think we should chuck the whole thing.

There is a pause. Suzi speaks with a quiet desperation.

SUZI: That's not fair... I don't - we all -

MANDY: You're in here every spare minute. Running to Miss Harper. 'Miss, I've had an idea for my magazine.' I reckon you sleep

67

in here. Some of us have got homes to go to you know. Just because your mum doesn't care whether you go home or not...

There is a pause, then a general murmur of disapproval.

(*Over-riding the others*) Going on as if it was her magazine and the rest of us just - her slaves.

SUZI: That's not true -

MANDY: All right then. I want to know why you've altered everything in my article.

SUZI: I didn't -

MANDY: Yes you did.

SUZI: I just - corrected a few spelling mistakes- and - and - where you'd written things - a bit wrong.

MANDY: Oh did you? I'm sorry I'm so pig-ignorant.

SUZI: It's what editors are supposed to do.

SIMON: I did some of it -

SUZI: You didn't -

SIMON: (*Ignoring Suzi*) You'd look pretty stupid if we printed exactly what you wrote.

MANDY: Trust you to stick up for her. How would you like it if she mucked up what you wrote?

GEMMA: Yes!

SIMON: Shut up, pea-brain.

MANDY: Well, I think Charlotte's right. I think we should stop now.

SUZI: (*Desperately*) No. Come on everybody. We've got a lot to do. All of us!

MANDY: You've got a lot to do you mean. I'm not bothering any more. You can do it on your own. I'm not wasting any more of my time. Coming, Gemma?

GEMMA: Yes, I am!

SIMON: Oh no! Gemma! Without your mighty brain we are lost!

MANDY: You can talk. You were supposed to be editor as well as her. How much editing do you do?

SIMON: (*Loftily*) I act in an advisory capacity.

MANDY: Yes because you're too lazy to do anything but talk. Like all boys. Dead lazy and all mouth.

ANTHONY: That's good. From you. Can I have a page of cartoons in the next magazine? I've done a great one of Mandy.

> *He holds out a sketch. Mandy takes it and tears it to shreds.*

ANTHONY: Don't you dare do that again. I'll get you for that. You just wait!

> *Tim takes a photograph. Mandy and Anthony turn on him. There is an outburst from them all.*

ANTHONY: Stop it, will you!

MANDY: I'm sick of you taking photos all the time!

TIM: It's for the magazine.

MANDY: There isn't going to be a magazine.

KEVIN: Not unless I find that £7.10.

JULIE: Oh stop being stupid.

ANGELA: I've got to go. I'm sick of all this rowing.

MANDY: I'm not stopping here.

GEMMA: Nor me.

> *Simon looks at Suzi who is sitting with her head in her hands.*

SIMON: Shut up! The lot of you!!!

> *Suzi looks up. She is very distressed.*

SUZI: If it's what you all want... I'll resign as editor. I - I think we should carry on with the magazine because - because - it's - good - and - and I think it's important. (*She is close to tears*) If you don't want me I'll - I'll go.

MANDY: All together now. Aaaah!

SUZI: Simon can be editor -

GEMMA: What about Mandy?

MANDY: Shut up!!

There is a tense pause. Everyone is uncomfortably aware that things can only get worse.

SIMON: I don't want to be editor. (*Looking at Mandy*) I suppose you want to do it.

MANDY: Me? I wouldn't waste my time. I've got better things to do than muck about with a stupid little comic.

SUZI: Have you done all this just to get at me?

MANDY: Why should I bother? You're not worth the trouble.

SUZI: You - I know what you're doing... You're - you were supposed to be my friend. But you can't stand it if anybody else does anything can you? You like to stand about and talk and bitch about everybody. But you never do anything yourself, do you? You just get at everybody else and cause trouble. You're poisonous!

MANDY: That's good from you! We all know why your Dad ran off and your Mum doesn't want you in the house. Nobody can stand you. Not even your own Mother!

SUZI: You're just a scheming little bitch...

The others are shocked into silence.

Where's that paper? (*Pause*) Come on, Simon. You know. That 'article' my friend Mandy wrote about me. Give it to me and I'll read it out aloud so everybody knows what she's like.

Suzi scarcely knows what she is doing.

SIMON: You don't want to read that. It's just - vile.

SUZI: Oh yes I do. I've got a right. It's about me isn't it?

MANDY: You wouldn't dare,

SUZI: Oh yes I would. Please, Simon. Give it to me.

SIMON: I am as much editor as you are. That was a nasty bit of rubbish from Mandy. And I'm censoring it.

He takes the paper from his pocket and tears it up into very small pieces which he puts in his mouth, chews up and spits out.

There. It doesn't exist now.

GEMMA: Ugh! That's disgusting...

There is a buzz of conversation and excited chatter.

SIMON: Come on. All of you. Out. We'll have another meeting later to decide what we do - That's it. Meeting over. I'm going to play table tennis.

MANDY: What makes you think you can order everybody about?

SIMON: Goodbye, Mandy. See you Monday.

Mandy looks at him and laughs.

MANDY: You're pathetic. Come on, Gemma.

Mandy and Gemma go out. Suzi has her head in her hands not looking at anyone. Simon gestures to the others over her head to go. With some reluctance and resignation they go, muttering, 'Bye, see you.' etc. Suzi does not look up.

SUZI: You might as well go. I can tell Miss Harper what's happened.

SIMON: We're joint editors.

SUZI: You didn't need to chew up that thing Mandy did.

SIMON: It wasn't up to our standards. Mandy isn't as clever as she likes to think.

SUZI: Mandy likes smashing things up.

SIMON: She only did it to be spiteful.

Suzi has begun to cry, but is determined not to show it.

SUZI: What's it got to do with you anyway?

SIMON: I didn't like it. (*Pause*) You going on the bus?

SUZI: Home! Huh! No.

SIMON: You walking then?

SUZI: Might.

SIMON: Come and have a game of table tennis.

SUZI: No. Thanks. (*Pause*) Stop trying to be nice to me. Why don't you just go off with the others. You don't like me either. Why don't you just go and leave me?

SIMON: You can't stop here.

SUZI: I'll do some work on the magazine then, won't I? There's plenty to do. Mandy Alfreds needn't think she can stop me.

SIMON: I'll help you.

SUZI: Please yourself.

> *She sits on the floor as she did at the beginning, head down, not looking at him.*

Don't interrupt me. I'm busy.

> *Simon stares at her for a moment then crosses to the door. He looks out into the corridor. Then closes the door firmly and crosses and sits at the table upstage of Suzi. She does not look at him. He picks up a magazine from the table and glances at it. He looks up and stares reflectively at Suzi. The lights fade.*

THE END

IN SERVICE

CHARACTERS

BETSY

DAISY

LAVINIA

EMILY

JESSIE

ALBERT

The play is set in the attic and the kitchen of a large house in the 1890s.

IN SERVICE

It is dawn in the attic of a large Victorian house. The grey light filters through the tiny, grimy and un-curtained skylight. There are four plain iron bedsteads, close together side by side. Downstage, between the beds, is a little wooden table. On it stands a single candlestick with a stub of candle in it, and a large jug and wash basin. Over the basin is draped a torn scrap of linen which serves as a towel. A fifth, makeshift, truckle bed has been pushed in at the foot of the bed nearest to the door. Three of the beds are occupied. Daisy, Emily and Betsy are all fast asleep wrapped up in rough patched blankets. It is very cold.

The attic occupies one main area of the stage. The other area represents the scullery, a bleak outhouse leading off from the kitchen. A large table with four or five chairs round it, stands centre suggesting the kitchen. Jessie is sitting, her legs drawn up, her head on her knees, on the scullery floor in front of the boiler

Lavinia - in the attic - is kneeling at the foot of the truckle bed. She is fast asleep, her head bowed over her clasped hands. She is fully dressed. There is a candlestick on the floor beside her. The candle has burnt out. Somewhere in the distance a church clock strikes six. Daisy wakes abruptly and sits up, yawning and clutching her blanket round her. She is also fully dressed except for her cap, apron and boots. She is a lively, energetic, fourteen year old. She gets out of bed and crosses to the wash-stand. Betsy, woken by her movements, yawns, stretches, but stays in her bed. She too is fourteen. Usually a cheerful and resourceful girl, at the moment she is very tired.

BETSY: I can't get up yet. I've only just gone to sleep.

DAISY: (*Picking up the water-jug*) Brr, it's cold. The water's frozen again.

She picks up the candlestick and attempts to break the ice with it.

DAISY: Oh, it's no good. It's too thick to break... Oh well. That's me not washed for another day!

BETSY: (*Chuckling*) You'd better not let Emily hear you. She'll tell them downstairs then you'll be for it.

DAISY: (*Pulling on her boots*) By the time I've black-leaded the grate nobody'll know whether I've washed or not.

> *Betsy gets up and stretches, then quickly puts on a big sacking apron which reaches to the ground. She too has slept in her clothes.*

BETSY: Ooooh! It is cold! You wouldn't like to do the front step for me would you? And I'll do the grate.

DAISY: No thank you, Betsy.

> *Betsy has become aware of Lavinia for the first time. She crosses to Daisy, giggling.*

BETSY: What's the matter with her?

> *Daisy giggles.*

DAISY: Saying a few prayers for us!

> *Daisy crosses to Lavinia and shouts 'Boo' suddenly at her. Lavinia starts awake and stares, uncomprehendingly, at Daisy for a moment. Then she looks round and realizes where she is. She begins to get painfully to her feet, stamping her foot on the floor and shivering.*

LAVINIA: Oh, I'm stiff! My foot's gone to sleep.

BETSY: So's the rest of you! What you doing - saying an extra long prayer?

> *Daisy and Betsy giggle.*

LAVINIA: (*Rubbing her ankle*) Yes - No - I mean, I was - I must have fallen asleep.

BETSY: Last night?

LAVINIA: Yes.

> *She bends painfully to pick up the candle*

DAISY: Did you let that candle just burn itself out?

LAVINIA: I - must have done... I don't remember. I just came up here...

And - I remember kneeling down to say my prayers - and I must have fallen asleep. Oh, I am stiff!

DAISY: Well, that's God punishing you for falling asleep when you should have been talking to Him.

BETSY: Daisy!

DAISY: I've got a special arrangement with God. I say my prayers in bed and he lets me off cleaning the saucepans.

BETSY: Daisy! Don't!

EMILY: (*Sleepily*) I wish you'd be quiet, Daisy. Some of us don't have to get up for another half an hour. I could get some more rest if you weren't tramping around making all that noise.

DAISY: Sorry Ma'am!

Lavinia has crossed to the water jug and is standing looking worriedly at it.

EMILY: What's the matter with you?

Her tone is slightly hostile. She gets out of bed. She is the only one who has not gone to bed in her clothes. She is dressed in her bodice and petticoat. She begins to get dressed, only half listening to what the others are saying.

LAVINIA: I fell asleep by the side of the bed. I was so tired...

EMILY: You'll get used to it.

Lavinia stares at the window which is downstage centre. After a moment she takes the chair and stands on it trying to look out, but the little skylight is too high for her to see anything. Betsy and Daisy nudge each other and giggle at her.

EMILY: (*Irritably*) What are you doing now?

LAVINIA: (*Climbing down quickly*) Nothing. I just wondered if you could see out at all.

DAISY: Course you can't! Anyway, what do you want to see out for? There's nothing out there - only the other side of the square, and you can see that from the front door.

LAVINIA: I like the open air. I don't like to be shut in...

BETSY: If you want to see outside you can do the front step.

Daisy giggles.

LAVINIA: It - makes me feel - I can't seem to breathe with all these buildings shutting me in.

There is a slight pause. The others stare at her as if she is a creature from another planet. Lavinia is embarrassed by their stares, as she realises they do not know what she is talking about. She quickly changes the subject.

LAVINIA: I'd better not do the step... I've got to do the pots and pans.

DAISY: The pots and pans! Oh the pots and pans!! Are you going to do them in the fresh air like the gyppoes on the Heath. Is that where you come from?

LAVINIA: No... I'm just - not used to the town... I was in a big house near Reading before... The sun came in through the window first thing in the morning and you could see right out over the fields...

DAISY: (*Aggressively*) Well, there's nothing like that here. You don't have fields in the middle of London. Hyde Park's better than any old fields... Where is Reading anyway? Sounds peculiar to me.

LAVINIA: (*Faltering*) It's - it's - in the country. But it's a town as well.

DAISY: How can you have a town in the country?

BETSY: What did you come here for?

LAVINIA: (*Wretchedly*) Mrs Granby - that's the lady where I was - is Lady Beesley's sister... She said I was a good reliable girl - I was a nursery maid and she... she used to give us lessons...

BETSY: (*Incredulously*) Herself?

LAVINIA: Yes. We all had to read the Bible and... poems... Good poems, about good things. Because she says a lot of poems are wicked. And - and she thinks we should find out about the way other people live and look after them... That's why she made me come here... to live in London, I mean... She wants some of (*She pauses and then goes on carefully*) - some of Lady Beesley's servants to go and live in the country...

There is a stunned pause.

DAISY: Well! I'd run away first. There's plenty of work round here. I'm not going to no country. Born and bred in London I am and I'm not leaving.

EMILY: There won't be anything like that here. Lady Beesley doesn't go interfering with us, reading the Bible and such like. We just go to prayers every day and Church on Sundays and that's it.

BETSY: Your Lady sounds a bit cracked to me.

LAVINIA: No. She had - beliefs she said. She thought you should treat servants properly...

DAISY: Ha! Well, I don't call that treating folks properly. Making you read the Bible and go and live in the country.

BETSY: I don't think it's right. Interfering like that. We've got our lives and they've got theirs.

EMILY: (*Thoughtfully*) Miss Augusta's a bit - she might go and do something like that. When I was carrying the coals up to the drawing room the other morning, she asked me if I said my own prayers every day.

DAISY: What did you say?

EMILY: I said yes and she gave me this.

She fishes under her blanket and produces a pamphlet.

DAISY: What is it?

EMILY: (*Vaguely*) A book - about being good.

LAVINIA: Mrs Granby used to have those. They're all about Jesus and somebody called Martha and being a good servant. You're supposed to be cheerful all the time and do your work for God and then scrubbing the floor's as good as going to Church.

DAISY: Sounds daft! Being cheerful don't get the front step any cleaner!

BETSY: No! In fact, I get it a lot cleaner if I'm in a really bad mood when I do it.

EMILY: (*Who is now fully dressed*) Mrs Bowler'll be in a really bad mood if you don't get down and get on with it. You should have been downstairs ten minutes ago!

She looks at Lavinia with open hostility.

EMILY: Are they going to make you a nursery maid here?

LAVINIA: I - don't know...

EMILY: You'd better not be, because I don't want to get sent into the country. I like it here. So you just keep quiet and make sure you get those saucepans so shiny they keep you in the kitchen! And don't leave candles burning in here all night again. You'll set us all on fire.

> *She turns away, as if to go out, then stops and straightens the blanket on her bed. Lavinia watches her, slightly afraid, and automatically copies her.*

BETSY: (*Jeering*) Didn't you sleep in a bed in the country? Slept in a barn did you? I'll get some straw from the street and you can root around in that tonight. There might be the odd bit of horse muck in it but I expect you're used to that. Come on, Daisy.

> *She and Daisy go out giggling. Lavinia and Emily are left facing each other.*

LAVINIA: Why are you all being so horrible to me? I didn't want to come here you know...

EMILY: Well, you better just keep quiet about it, hadn't you? And don't go boasting about the country and fields and what a good steady girl you are... and showing off about reading because that's not the way we are in London.

> *She goes out leaving Lavinia biting her lip. After a moment she follows Emily out.*
>
> *The attention shifts to the scullery and Jessie who stands up, stretches and yawns. She then shakes her head and begins to rake out the ashes and lay and light the boiler. Lavinia comes slowly into the scullery. Jessie sits back on her heels and looks at her. Jessie has a sharp tongue, but is a kind-hearted girl. She is a little older than the others and rather more thoughtful.*

JESSIE: Come on - Look sharp! Where've you been? I want to get started on the breakfasts. I need those pans.

LAVINIA: They are clean. I did them yesterday.

JESSIE: What's your name again?

LAVINIA: Lavinia.

JESSIE: Funny sort of name.

LAVINIA: I'm sorry.

JESSIE: It's not your fault. Well, Lavinia, those saucepans aren't clean enough. They've got to be done again. Mrs Bowler likes those pans gleaming like gold before we're allowed to use them.

LAVINIA: Scour them again?

JESSIE: Yes. I don't know what you did in your last place but these slip-slop ways won't do here. That porridge pan's got a line round it. If Mrs Bowler sees that you'll be out on the streets, my girl!

LAVINIA: I'm sorry. I'm not used to pans.

JESSIE: (*Crossing to the table*) Well. You'd better get used to them. (*Kindly*) The thing to do is to clean them till you can see your face in them. Then start all over again. It's like this table. When I first came here I had to scrub it till my hands were raw. It has to be pure white, and not a speck of dust or dirt anywhere. They're very good here - you just do your work properly and you'll be all right. But they can't abide slovens.

> *Lavinia begins to scour out the vast black porridge pot. Emily comes in with an expression of extreme distaste on her face, leading in a deplorable, filthy urchin - Albert, the mudlark. He is a small, wiry, impudent-looking boy, liberally covered with mud. His clothes are a collection of unrecognizable rags. Barefooted, he stands in the middle of the room, looking round him, aggressively.*

JESSIE: Ugh! What's that? Don't put it there. I've just scrubbed that floor. Here. Stand on this paper, you!

> *She seizes some newspapers from a box by the boiler and crosses and puts them down for Albert to stand on. She does not touch him at all.*

JESSIE: Come on! On that paper! (*Threateningly as he does not move*) Do as you're told or you'll get a clip round the ear!

> *Albert decides not to risk it and steps resentfully onto the paper.*

JESSIE: Ugh! What a stink! What is all this, Emily?

She and Emily move away from Albert.

EMILY: He's a mudlark if you please. Miss Augusta found him. Don't ask me what she wants the horrible little object for. (*Turning to the boy*) You! What does she want you for?

Albert glowers at her but does not answer.

Did you hear me? I asked you a question.

Albert turns away from Emily. She picks up a ladle and begins to poke him with it.

EMILY: Did - you - hear - what - I - said? - Answer - your - betters - when - they - speak - to - you - Guttersnipe!

JESSIE: Don't do that, Em. I want that for the porridge. Look he's filthy. River mud all over him. You'll get diseases all over that ladle.

Emily continues, punctuating her words with vicious little digs with the ladle.

EMILY: I'll - teach - you - to - speak - when - you're - spoken - to! You - smelly - little - animal!

Goaded, the boy grabs the ladle and threatens Emily with it, growling menacingly.

EMILY: Oooh! Hark at him!

JESSIE: (*Taking the ladle* I'll have that. Look at it - it's filthy!

EMILY: (*Gesturing at Lavinia*) She can clean it. Here. Come on! Take it. There's some nice fresh outdoor mud for you. Ugh!

She wipes her hands together daintily. Daisy and Betsy, wearing vast sacking aprons, come in. Betsy is carrying a bucket of water and a large scrubbing brush. Daisy has a vast floor-mop. They stop dead at the sight of the boy

DAISY: Ugh! What's that?

BETSY: What's it doing here?

EMILY: It's a mudlark Miss Augusta found. She's brought it here for us to see to.

LAVINIA: (*Quietly to Jessie*) What's a mudlark?

JESSIE: Oh they're horrible things. There's hundreds of them down by the river. Mostly dirty little urchins like that but there's some old women as well. They go rooting round the mud at low tide, picking up bits of rubbish. Old bones, rusty nails and bits of coal. Then they sell them. Nasty, dirty, diseased things they are. (*To Emily*) What's Miss Augusta up to now?

EMILY: I don't know. Mrs Bowler just called me out of the nursery and said Miss Augusta brought him back last night. She'd been to some meeting with that fiancé of hers and they brought this back. Found it wandering around, pestering people, holding cab doors open for a penny. Looking for something to steal more like. Miss Augusta made it run back here back of the cab. It slept in the stables.

BETSY: What are we supposed to do with it?

EMILY: Mrs Bowler says we're to get the worst of the mud off, then she'll see if it can be put in the tin bath in the yard. She's not going to touch it till we've got rid of the mud and the stink.

DAISY: (*Handing her mop to Betsy*) I'm not touching that! I'm supposed to be black-leading the grate.

BETSY: I can't touch him with this. It'll ruin the mop.

EMILY: (*Pointing at Lavinia*) She can do it. She was a nursery maid at her old house. Here, get this bucket and scrubbing brush and clean it up!

BETSY: (*Giggling*) That water's filthy. I've just scrubbed the step with it.

EMILY: It's a lot cleaner than him. You don't want to waste clean water on that! (*To Lavinia*) Here you! Get on with it. You can use some of that scouring powder if you like.

JESSIE: What does Miss Augusta want him for?

EMILY: I don't know. Mrs Bowler says she's gone soft in the head. That fiancé of hers. He's trying to get in Parliament and he's got a lot of silly ideas about looking after the poor. They want to spend some time looking after decent, hard-working folk, not filthy little animals like that. (*Becoming aware that the boy is glaring at her with pure hatred*) You're a filthy - what are you?

DAISY: Even if you get him clean he'll only go stealing again. You can't do anything with creatures like that.

BETSY: Well, do you want this water or shall I tip it away?

EMILY: Come on. Get scrubbing. If he gives you any trouble hit him with the scrubbing brush. I'll go and tell Mrs Bowler. (*To Betsy*) You'd better go and get some fires lit upstairs or you'll be for it.

Emily goes out with a last disdainful grimace at Albert, who sticks his tongue out. Betsy takes off her apron and hands it to Lavinia. She sets the bucket and brush near Albert, puts away the mop and picks up a coal scuttle.

BETSY: You can wash that apron through when you've finished. I don't want mud all over it.

She goes out after Emily. Jessie lifts the large black kettle off the hob and pours some water into the bucket.

JESSIE: There you are. Have a bit of hot. That'll help get some of the mud off. That water's stone cold. I've got to take the hot water upstairs. I'll see if I can find you some old rags to dry him with.

She goes out, followed by Daisy.

DAISY: I'll be in the kitchen doing the grate. Don't let it run away. I'll come and black-lead it for you when you've finished.

The boy watches Lavinia, as she picks up the brush and puts some soap on it. She approaches Albert diffidently.

LAVINIA: I've got to get you clean. You will stand still, won't you? I won't hurt you.

Neither moves.

You can talk, can't you?

ALBERT: Course I can talk. Weren't gonna talk to them, was I?

LAVINIA: What's your name?

ALBERT: Albert. What's yours?

LAVINIA: Lavinia. (*Looking at him, biting her lip*) I don't know where to start. Are you dirty all over?

ALBERT: Yeah. You go in up to your knees this weather. I bin in up to me waist. I likes to nip in between the barges as well. That's where you get the best stuff. That's where you get the pitch all over you.

Lavinia stares at him not understanding.

Off of the barges... the pitch... off the bottoms. (*Looking interestedly at his arm*) That's horse muck from the stables that is!

LAVINIA: Look. I think you'd better let me tie this apron round you... then you can take those - rags off... and I can scrub you...

She ties the huge sacking apron round his neck so that he is enveloped in it from head to foot. His face peeping over the top, he looks as if he has been tied into a sack. Lavinia kneels at his feet and begins to scrub his legs, shyly pushing aside the sacking. Albert looks down with interest.

ALBERT: In the House of Correction they stood you in the yard and hosed you down. Knocked you off your feet that did.

LAVINIA: House of Correction? Have you been there?

ALBERT: Four times. I prigged some coal from the barges and they got me. I was looking for copper nails. They're the best but there wasn't none. Prison's all right in the winter. They give you shoes and a shirt. It's powerful hard on the feet in the winter. With the ice... And the broken glass. That's bad... There look. A broken bottle done that. Sliced through them toes. Still. If you ain't got no toes you can't get no chilblains.

LAVINIA: Oh dear. Did it hurt?

ALBERT: Course it did. But the mud blocked up the ends and I don't miss them toes now.

Lavinia draws back in horror from Albert's feet.

LAVINIA: Put your hands in this bucket and I can wash your arms.

Albert kneels down, putting his arms in the bucket, and passively allows her to wash his arms.

LAVINIA: Where do you live?

ALBERT: Back of King James Stairs. Down Wapping Wall. My mum sells fish down there. When she can. But she's been in the Fever Hospital a long time now. My Dad fell between the barges. Broke his back. Drunk as usual. So me and our Nellie went mudlarking. (*Proudly*) I get fourpence a day... you can, on a good day... If I could find a hammer or a saw I could get eightpence then we'd be all right. Will she - the Lady - will she, do you reckon, she'll give me some money?

LAVINIA: I don't know. She - she might want to teach you to read. But I expect she'll give you some food or clothes -

ALBERT: I know reading. Well I did. I was - Ow!

Lavinia has washed his face with the floor cloth. Albert comes up spluttering.

LAVINIA: That's better. (*Looking at him doubtfully*) You can read?

ALBERT: Well. I did once. One night I was down by the steam factory. The warm water runs out there and you can warm your feet up a bit, you see. These big lads was talking about the ragged school in the High Street. They said it was good fun - you had a good laugh, making game of the master, and that, and putting out the gas and chucking the slates about. They said there was a fire there. So I went along to have a warm. They used to give us tea parties and magic lantern shows. I got to like it so I went every night. They was mostly thieves that used to go. Thieving the coal and cutting the ropes off of the ships and selling it at the rag shops. We all used to go thieving after School. While we was waiting for the School doors to open we used to plan where we'd go. I got taken up for thieving coals. But they did reading. I never went back when I come out of prison.

LAVINIA: I shouldn't tell Miss Augusta about the thieving if I was you. I expect she'll want to read to you about Jesus and things.

ALBERT: I've heard tell of him. They've got him down the Catholic Church. They sometimes give you a bit of bread and say it's from Jesus, but I don't know.

LAVINIA: There that's a bit better. Don't take that apron off! I think Mrs Bowler can put you in the bath now. I've got the worst off. I'll get Emily.

ALBERT: Is that the snotty-faced one?

LAVINIA: Er. She's the one that brought you in.

ALBERT: I hate her.

LAVINIA: She's – she's not very kind...

She looks at him with sudden urgency.

Do you want to run away?

ALBERT: What for?

LAVINIA: Back to the river.

ALBERT: Nah. It's horrible. I'll get food and clothes here. I ain't had a decent feed for ages.

LAVINIA: But they'll scrub you and make you read books and say prayers and lock you up in a nasty cold room with just a little window and they'll be horrible to you - especially Emily. And *you* don't have to stay here...

ALBERT: That's better than Wapping Stairs. I don't mind being shut up and scrubbed if I can make a bit out of it.

LAVINIA: (*Wistfully*) I'd like to run away.

ALBERT: Yeah? What for?

LAVINIA: I don't like it in the town. I used to live in the country... You could walk over the fields... and pick flowers and - and climb up onto the haystack and watch the clouds...

ALBERT: That don't sound too healthy. You got your grub and a bed and some shoes. You hang onto 'em.

Emily comes back. She looks him up and down.

EMILY: Well, I suppose that'll do. Till Mrs Bowler gets at him. There'll be a mattress for him to sleep on, in the stables. Make sure he doesn't steal the spoons.

Daisy and Betsy return, carrying bowls of porridge. Jessie follows them with a large jug of milk and some bread. They set the food down on the table.

JESSIE: Breakfast. Come on, Lavinia...

The girls settle themselves at the table. Albert drifts nearer, attracted by the food. Lavinia stands, irresolute, in the middle of the scullery.

EMILY: You! Go and sit on that stool by the fire. As far away as you like. please.

Albert scuttles over to the fire, anxious to get some breakfast. Jessie takes him a bowl of porridge and a piece of bread.

DAISY: Put it on the floor. Let him lap it up like a dog. Don't let him dirty a spoon.

Albert takes the bowl and the bread and scoops up the porridge, half drinking it, half mopping it up with the bread. Betsy and Daisy laugh at him. Emily watches him with disgust. Lavinia turns away from the table and watches him sadly.

DAISY: Hey! Daydream! Do you want your breakfast on the floor as well?

Lavinia crosses to the table and sits by herself. The other girls sit close together, eating their breakfast and giggling. Jessie watches Lavinia curiously. Lavinia looks at Albert, sighs, glances at the others, smiles weakly at Jessie and looks down at her porridge. She then clasps her hands together and closes her eyes.

LAVINIA: 'For what we are about to receive may the Lord make us truly grateful for the sake of Jesus Christ our Lord. Amen.'

The lights fade

THE END

THE COLOUR OF COMPASSION
THE STORY OF
MARY SEACOLE

CHARACTERS

MARY SEACOLE
LITTLE MARY
MARY'S MOTHER
BESSIE
WOMAN WITH BABY
WOMAN WITH CHOLERA
SISTER-IN-LAW
FIRST, SECOND, THIRD & FOURTH AMERICAN WOMAN
STEWARDESS
MISS JELKES
MRS STANLEY
MRS HERBERT
MAIDSERVANT
MRS BRACEBRIDGE
FLORENCE NIGHTINGALE
FIRST & SECOND LADY
DR. BARRY
YOUNG WIFE
NURSE
EMILY
SARAH
SILENT MAN

The play is set in Kingston, Jamaica; Panama; London and the Crimea in the early to mid nineteenth century.

The play was devised and performed by a group of nine actors, onstage throughout, but can be played by as many actors as there are characters.

THE COLOUR OF COMPASSION
THE STORY OF
MARY SEACOLE

The stage is in darkness. Music is heard faintly. A military march, fading into a scarcely defined Caribbean sound. We hear birdsong, exotic, tropical sounds and an underlying rumble of gunfire.

The lights come up so that we can see a desk upstage centre with a quill pen on it, a chair and a screen. On the floor are eight dull grey blankets lying in neat rows.

Mary Seacole and Florence Nightingale, the lady with the lamp, who remains motionless, upstage, enter together. Mary moves slowly towards the desk and sits down. She has a shawl round her head and shoulders. She takes up her pen and begins to write. As her voice is heard the rest of the cast enters slowly. The women are dressed in long dresses, their heads are bowed. They move slowly to the blankets and sit down. The male cast member lies down upstage, his back to the audience.

MARY: (*Voice Over*) 'I was born in the town of Kingston, in the island of Jamaica... I am a Creole and have good Scotch blood coursing in my veins. My father was a soldier of an old Scotch family and to him I often trace my affection for a camp-life and my sympathy with "the pomp, pride and circumstance of glorious war..." My mother kept a boarding house in Kingston, and was an admirable doctoress in high repute with the officers of both services and their wives who were stationed in Kingston. And so I had from early youth a yearning for medical knowledge and practice which has never deserted me.'

The music/soundtrack is louder now. In the semi-darkness, hushed and as if coming from a long way away, the women on the blankets begin to speak, sometimes together, and at other times, individually. As they are speaking Florence Nightingale moves forwards, her lamp held high and moves slowly round the stage from bed to bed. She puts the lamp down on Mary's desk as the women finish speaking, and goes and sits, downstage right.

VOICES: Dame Seacole was a kindly old soul,
And a kindly old soul was she;
You might call for your pot you may call for your pipe
In her tent on the 'Col' so free.

Her tent on the 'Col' where a welcome toll
She took of the passing throng,
That from Balaclava to the front
Toiled wearily along.

That berry-brown face with a kind heart's trace
Impressed in each wrinkle sly,
Was a sight to behold though the snow-clouds rolled
Across that iron sky.

The music fades and we are left with the birdsong. Mary looks up, puts down her pen and takes off her shawl.

MARY: When I was a young girl in Jamaica I dreamed of being a qualified doctoress. I knew it was impossible, but I was determined to try. I watched my mother, day by day, for she was a healer.

She gets up and moves away from the desk and goes towards the beds. The lights come up full on the female figures on the beds. They are all lying, sitting, lolling about like broken dolls.

MARY: My favourite game was nursing my dolls back to health.

She moves from bed to bed, lifting up the dolls' heads and administering 'medicine' to them.

MARY: (*To the first 'doll'*) Oh dear, what's the matter with you - a fever? You're burning! Here, swallow this. The herbs and the honey will soon bring your temperature down.

The doll sits up with a bright smile. Then as Mary moves on to the next bed she gets up and crosses upstage and stands watching Mary with a little smile on her face. She is now Mary's mother.

MARY: (*To the second doll*) Come along. Sit up. Just you eat this nice guava jelly and you'll be as right as rain.

Sorrowfully she lays down the third doll, closing its eyes.

Oh no. Oh dear. My favourite girl... (*Sternly to the last doll*) Come on sit up. There's nothing the matter with you! I know you and your tricks. On your feet.

MOTHER: Mary Jane Grant! What are you doing? Are you playing with those dolls again? Just you come here and get on with your tasks. That's all you ever do!

MARY: I have to practise. I'm going to be a doctoress and heal people like you do...

MOTHER: You are going to be a nice well brought up, well-mannered young lady, first of all, and you don't do that by playing with dolls. Now. Inside with you and help me. If you want to be like me you're going to have to work with all your might. Go on, off with you.

Mary goes back to her desk. The mother back to her bed. Music plays quietly. Mary is isolated at her desk in a pool of light. She takes up her pen again.

MARY: (*Voice Over*) 'Before long it was very natural that I should extend my practice; and so I found other patients in the dogs and cats around me. Many luckless brutes had forced down their reluctant throats the remedies I deemed most likely to suit their supposed complaints. And after a time I rose still higher in my ambition; and despairing of finding another human patient, I proceeded to try my simples and essences upon - myself.'

During this speech Mary acts out what she is describing, with one of the cast playing the cat. She finally returns to her desk and swallows a glass of fearsome looking liquid. She shudders and checks her pulse.

Little Mary rises and crosses to the desk. Mary Seacole is writing now. She does not look up. Little Mary moves closer to the desk. She is still standing just outside the light.

LITTLE MARY: Do you remember me, Miss Mary?

Mary Seacole looks up, holding her quill pen raised above the paper. She does not look at Little Mary.

MARY: Little Mary. Yes I remember.

She stares into the distance. Her mother rises and circles round the desk. She too stands in the shadows.

MOTHER: Mary. You can't go on like this. You're not a child... it's time you time you grew up and faced your responsibilities. Time you were married. A very fine man, Mr Seacole, has asked for you. He's a good quiet man. He's not very strong - his health is delicate but he'll make you a good husband. And you've learned enough from me to be able to take good care of him.

MARY: (*Not looking at her mother*) But I hardly know him.

MOTHER: Time to get to know him after you're married.

Mother moves away and stands further upstage turned away from them. Little Mary crouches beside the desk.

LITTLE MARY: Are you going away, Miss Mary?

MARY: Yes, Little Mary. I'm going to be married.

LITTLE MARY: I wish you weren't going away. I shall miss you...

Mary Seacole crosses, decisively, centre stage.

MARY: Mother! If I'm to be married, I'd like Little Mary to come with me. A married lady should have her own servant. (*To Little Mary*) Would you like that?

LITTLE MARY: Oh yes please!

MARY: May she, Mother?

MOTHER: Well... yes... I suppose I can spare her.

Mary Seacole and Little Mary move away upstage towards the desk. Mary Seacole sits down. Little Mary moves towards the upstage right blanket where the male figure is lying. Mother moves downstage and stands with her back to the stage. Bessie, her servant, gets up and brings her a chair. She sits down rather wearily, holding her hand to her head. Bessie has a large shopping basket.

MARY: So I married Mr Seacole. He was a good man but very weak and sickly. My medicines that worked so well with my dolls, and all the skills I'd learned from my mother weren't enough to save him.

BESSIE: What am I to fetch, mam?

MOTHER: (*Wearily*) Just a minute Bessie, I need to... My head's so muzzy I can't think straight.

Little Mary is bending over the man placing her hand on his head. She is very worried.

LITTLE MARY: Miss Mary... Mrs Seacole... Can you come here? Mr Seacole... he's very fevered... I can't wake him up.

Mary Seacole gets up from her desk and crosses and kneels beside her husband. She very expertly takes his pulse, etc. She gets to her feet decisively.

MARY: Yes. You're right. He has a very bad fever. He won't get well here. We're too near the river. The fever breeds on that water. Run to my mother and ask if I can bring him to her house. If we get him away from this sickly air we can save him.

Little Mary crosses to Bessie and her mother. The little group freezes.

MARY: But I couldn't save him....

She kneels down and closes his eyes. She gets up slowly and walks across to the other group.

BESSIE: She's really bad, Miss Mary. Can't think what she wants from the market and when I ask her what I'm to get for dinner she just sighs and says, 'Oh do what you like, Bessie, I don't want anything.'

MARY: (*Slowly*) Any more than I could save my dear mother. Her time came all too soon after my husband. Nothing I could do, nothing I tried, could save either of them.

She closes her mother's eyes. Bessie and Little Mary go back to their places. The lights fade on the mother. Music plays and she slowly returns to her place. Mary Seacole returns to her desk and picks up her pen.

MARY: I was alone in the world. Except for my faithful Little Mary. There was nothing to keep me in Jamaica. I had lost my mother and my husband...The cleverest doctors in the world cannot fight off Death when it is his time. I could not stay - alone - where there were so many memories. And so I set sail for South America - to my brother, in Panama, where I could use my skills saving sick folk who weren't ready for death...

Mary rises and crosses centre stage. A woman, carrying a baby, rises and meets her. She holds out the baby to Mary and watches anxiously as Mary takes it. The rest of the cast turn and lie in different attitudes on their blankets. Little Mary is ministering to them. A cloaked and hooded male figure stands upstage, his back to the audience, holding a spade.

WOMAN: Mother Seacole... the baby... this child... my neighbour's boy... he's very sick... please... can you save him?

Mary slowly takes the baby from her and glances at it.

MARY: (*In a quiet unemotional voice*) Cholera.

WOMAN: No. No. It's just a baby sickness... not cholera, not this baby... he's too little...

MARY: No-one is too little - or too old. Where is his mother? Why have you brought him to me?

WOMAN: His mother is dead. She was all he had. She was lying dead on the floor with him in her arms. There was no-one else in the house. All dead. You can make him better... There is no-one like... no-one like... You have cured so many people. You know what to do.

MARY: And so many have died... He is very little. I will do what I can.

WOMAN: You must. I can't keep this child - (*Gesturing to the invalids*) These people. You've cured them.

Little Mary gently pulls a blanket up over the face of one of the patients. Then rises and goes and stands beside Mary.

MARY: Some of them... Leave the child with me. I'll see what I can do. The rest of your family... Has the cholera struck any of them?

The woman looks at her in terror and turns away.

MARY: Well?

WOMAN: (*Almost inaudibly*) My husband... my sister... her two daughters...

MARY: Did nobody survive?

WOMAN: My brother... And I am... well..

WOMAN PATIENT: Thirsty... So thirsty... something to drink...

MARY: (*Calling across to Little Mary*) Give her some cinnamon water.

She crosses to the woman and feels her head.

She needs another mustard poultice to her spine and her neck... We must keep her warm around her heart... And every quarter of an hour we must give her ten grains of sugar of lead mixed in water.

Little Mary fetches the cinnamon water, gently raises the patient and gives her some to drink. Mary turns back to the woman with the baby.

MARY: Give me the baby.

She takes the baby and looks down at it sadly.

Leave him with me. And go back to your home - while you are still healthy. Cholera is in the air you breathe and everything you touch here. I will do what I can for this child. But it may be that all I can do is pray.

The woman goes sadly away. Mary sits with the baby in her lap. Little Mary and one of the women bring across a screen which they place in front of the patients. Mary is sitting in front of it. The lights lower, and there is a red flickering light on Mary and the baby.

MARY: (*Voice Over*) 'So the long night passed away; first a death-like stillness behind one screen, and then a sudden silence behind the other, showing that the fierce battle with death was over. And I sat with my last patient in my lap - a poor little brown-faced orphan, scarce a year old was dying in my arms and I was powerless to save it. I thought more of that child than of the men who were struggling for their lives and prayed earnestly to God to spare it. But it did not please Him to grant my prayer and towards morning the wee spirit left this sinful world and what was mortal of the little infant lay dead in my arms.'

Little Mary comes forward and takes the baby away

> *upstage pulling the blanket over its head. She gives it to the hooded man, who takes it, roughly, and remains motionless. She then returns and lies down near to where Mary is sitting, lost in thought.*

MARY: What did he say?

LITTLE MARY: He will bury him at dawn. With the others.

MARY: Are there many others to bury?

LITTLE MARY: (*Sleepily*) No. There are no others to bury tomorrow... He means he'll put him in the same grave... .he's the only one tomorrow...

> *She is almost asleep.*

MARY: The only one... I wonder... an orphan... nobody will be there for his funeral except - His family are all dead of the cholera... his poor little body will be put into the ground with no-one to weep for him... Mary... an idea has come into my mind... a frightening idea... Mary?... asleep... so I'm talking to myself... What if I took this child and examined it... I could learn more about this terrible disease... There is nothing more that I can do for my baby patient... I have done all I can for him in this life... but if by cutting open his body I could find out more... could save others... He has no need now of his body... Why bury it just to rot...?

> *The lights change. Little Mary and the other patients are still sleeping. Mary rises and crosses to the cloaked figure of the man who has the body of the child. They speak together unheard by the audience. Mary gives him some money and they move away upstage behind the screen.*

MARY: (*Voice Over*) 'It was cold grey dawn and the rain had ceased, when I followed the man who had taken the dead child to bury it and bribed him to carry it by an unfrequented path down to the riverside... and he stayed by me and aided me in my first and last post-mortem examination. We buried the poor little body beneath a piece of luxuriant turf and stole back like guilty things. But the knowledge I obtained was very valuable to me and was soon put into practice.'

> *Mary moves back to her desk and stands behind it turning*

over the pages of her book, as if reminding herself of what she has already done with her life and what she has written.

MARY: That was when I first became famous. I built a hotel in Panama where I looked after all sorts of folk. Word got around. Everybody knew Mother Seacole would cure you of all your sicknesses and then take fine care of you... But I was getting restless again.

Mary moves towards centre stage where her sister-in-law rises and crosses to meet her.

MARY: Well, I reckon that you and my brother will make a good job of running my hotel. It's all yours now.

SISTER-IN-LAW: I wish you weren't going. We'll never be able to manage the way you do...

MARY: No, I'm sure you won't. But there aren't as many sick folks here now as there used to be. I've cured 'em all! I'm tired to death of Panama. I'm going home to Kingston. And I'm catching the first steamer that leaves Navy Bay.

SISTER-IN-LAW: (*Warning*) That's an American ship -

MARY: Yes.

SISTER-IN-LAW: Don't sail on that ship, Mary... Wait till the English company's steamer calls...

MARY: Now why would I want to do that? It might be weeks and there's a steamer waiting to sail...

SISTER-IN-LAW: Mr... what's his name.. that American friend of yours... He doesn't think you should go on an American ship.

MARY: And did he say why I shouldn't?

SISTER-IN-LAW: No...but... He's a merchant... his business is in Navy Bay. He knows about ships...

MARY: I know. He's told me a dozen times not to take the American boat. But he can't give me a good reason. So I'm not waiting a minute longer. I'm going back to Jamaica by the first boat leaving here.

Music. Sea music. American in feeling. A very grand

American woman and her two daughters move upstage to a higher level and stand looking down, as if from the deck of a ship. A fourth woman joins them. A ship's officer is standing a little way away from them. Mary Seacole moves out from behind her desk and moves downstage. Little Mary rises and comes across to her carrying their luggage, which she sets down. The two Marys are standing downstage, looking up at the ship. The four American women move down towards them as they begin to move up the gangplank, and block their way.

FIRST WOMAN: Where are you going?

MARY: To Kingston.

FIRST WOMAN: And how are you going?

MARY: By sea.

FIRST WOMAN: Don't be impertinent, yaller woman. By what conveyance are you going?

MARY: By this steamer of course. I've paid for my passage.

SECOND WOMAN: Guess a yaller woman don't go along with us in this saloon.

THIRD WOMAN: I never travelled with the likes of her yet and I expect I shan't begin now.

While this is going on, a small group circles round Little Mary and, quietly, begin to pinch and push her around.

MARY: (*Voice Over*) 'Some children had taken my little servant Mary in hand and were practising on her the politeness which their parents were favouring me with. Only as is the wont of children, they were crueller. I cannot help it if I shock my readers: but the truth is that one positively spat in poor little Mary's frightened yellow face.'

FOURTH WOMAN: (*To Mary Seacole*) Well, now, I tell you for your good, you'd better quit this, and not drive my people to extremities. If you do you'll be sorry for it I expect.

MARY: Stewardess!!

A tall thin woman comes across. She and Mary Seacole move a little way away from the others.

MARY: My good woman, put me anywhere - under a boat - in your store-room, so that I can get to Kingston somehow.

STEWARDESS: There's nowhere but the saloon, and you can't expect to stay with the white people that's clear. Flesh and blood can stand a good deal of aggravation; but not that. If the Britishers is so took up with coloured people that's their business; but it won't do here.

MARY: Mary. Bring our things over here. We shall speak to the captain.

STEWARDESS: He won't tell you anything different. He'll give you your money back but this boat's leaving and you're staying here.

The cast move away to the upper level and line up, as if by the ship's rail, and look down at the two Marys standing with their luggage round them. Music and the ship's siren sound. The cast move back to their places. Little Mary picks up the luggage and takes it away upstage.

MARY: So the American ship sailed without us. Two days later we sailed for Jamaica on an English ship. They were politer. That wonderful English politeness that never comes right out and says what they mean. But goes on thinking it just the same... I stayed in Jamaica for eight months.

Little Mary comes forward with a large map, with a red cross chalked on it. She props it against the desk and Mary Seacole stands in front of it, lost in thought.

Silently and efficiently the other women move round and turn back the blankets and smooth them out carefully on the floor, on the upper level. The other sides of the blankets are clean and white. Florence Nightingale moves forward and watches as the 'beds' are put in place. A wounded man is helped into one of the beds. Florence Nightingale moves and stands beside him with her back to the audience. She is holding her lamp.

LITTLE MARY: Where's that place with the cross? Is it Panama?

MARY: No. That's in Russia. That place is called the Crimea... And this is England.

LITTLE MARY: I know that.

There is a pause as Mary Seacole is lost in thought again. Little Mary is beginning to feel worried.

LITTLE MARY: Why do you keep staring at that place? Do you want to go there?

MARY: More than anything else in the world.

LITTLE MARY: What for ?

MARY: There's a terrible war. Here. The English and the French have declared war on the Russians. To help the Turks. The Russians have been over-running the Turkish lands...

Her voice is far away. She is not really thinking about Little Mary.

As the scene continues, Mrs Herbert's home is set up. Mrs Elizabeth Herbert is sitting in her drawing room, with Mary Stanley and Miss Jelkes, a nursing recruit. Her maidservant is in the entrance hall and her footman stands by the door.

MARY: There are hundreds... No, thousands, of brave young soldiers fighting and dying on those battlefields. And there are thousands more dying from cholera and dysentery... and festering wounds... because there is no-one to care for them... No. There is one person. Miss Nightingale. She has done battle with the men in charge and taken some brave women out to the Crimea to nurse those poor boys...

LITTLE MARY: Is it very far away?

MARY: From here? Yes a very long way... I shall have to go to London first...

LITTLE MARY: Are we going to England then?

MARY: We? Will you come with me, Little Mary?

LITTLE MARY: Oh yes. Of course I will.

MARY: It's autumn in England now. It's cold and damp and foggy.

LITTLE MARY: I don't mind. What will you do?

MARY: I shall gather together all the testimonials to my skill as a doctoress that I have. I shall go to the War Office in London and then I will go to the war as one of Miss Nightingale's nurses. I'll be very useful because I have all the skills they need. I shall be more than a nurse. I shall help the doctors. I can cure cholera and dysentery... I'm famous as a doctoress everywhere in this latitude... I can heal wounds that other doctors have declared hopeless...

The two Marys move away from centre stage. and the attention shifts to Mrs Herbert's room.

MRS STANLEY: You will be paid twelve to fourteen shillings per week. You will be given a uniform, and board and lodging. If you complete a year's satisfactory service you will be paid twenty shillings per week.

MISS JELKES: The money is not important to me. I just want to go out there to help those brave, brave soldiers... To be able to comfort the dying -

MRS HERBERT: The money is important to Miss Nightingale. Miss Nightingale's nurses are not tender-hearted young novices. They are trained nurses who will obey orders - Miss Nightingale's orders - and will wear their uniform with pride and do as they are told at all times.

MISS JELKES: Oh, of course I understand... Is Miss Nightingale very strict?

MRS HERBERT: Very.

MRS STANLEY: She has already sent home five nurses. Almost as soon as they got there.

MISS JELKES: Oh dear. Why was that?

MRS STANLEY: Some were too old, some were drunkards, some were incompetent and some were thieves.

MRS HERBERT: A great many of the women were widows with large families to support and they were tempted by the money.

MISS JELKES: I am not married.

MRS STANLEY: No. That is in your favour. Do you have any experience of nursing?

MISS JELKES: Certainly not. I am a lady!

MRS STANLEY: (*Drily*) That is Miss Nightingale's problem. In her eyes nursing is an honourable profession. It is not a job - as it always has been for the raggle-taggle riff-raff who follow the soldiers wherever they go -

MISS JELKES: - I should hope not indeed. Miss Nightingale is also a lady -.

MRS HERBERT: (*Overriding her*) - Nor does she want ladies who will faint clean away at the sight of a gaping wound.

MRS STANLEY: Who think it's romantic to go to war and wipe away the blood with a little lace handkerchief.

MISS JELKES: I am young. I am well born. I wish to serve my country. I am ready to do what I can. I have no experience but I can learn.

MRS STANLEY: The other reason Miss Nightingale sends her nurses back is for 'impropriety of conduct.'

MISS JELKES: I hope you do not think I would be guilty of that!

MRS STANLEY: What do you think it means, Miss Jelkes?

MISS JELKES: Disgraceful... unladylike conduct... Vulgarity... or loud behaviour.

MRS STANLEY: No. More than that. It means disobeying Miss Nightingale. In the smallest detail.

The group freezes. Mary Seacole comes forward slowly, her papers in her hand. Little Mary comes to meet her, with a questioning look. Mary Seacole shakes her head wearily, crosses and sits at her desk, her head bowed.

MARY: (*Looking up angrily*) Forty six! Forty six more nurses are being sent out to join Miss Nightingale. I have spent twenty days crossing the Atlantic to be one of their number - and no-one will see me. I trail from office to office and nice gentlemanly young fellows look me up and down and tell me I have no chance. They hardly bother to hide their grins!! I have been shown the door in every room in the War Department - Little Mary!

LITTLE MARY: Are we going home?

MARY: No. We are not. I am going to Belgrave Square. If they won't see me in the War Department I shall go to the Secretary at

War's house. His wife is interviewing nurses for Miss Nightingale. She will see me.

Little Mary shakes her head sadly and goes to her place. Mary Seacole moves across and enters the hall of the house in Belgrave square, where the maidservant greets her.

MAIDSERVANT: Yes. What is it you want?

MARY: I must see Mrs Herbert.

MAIDSERVANT: Mrs Herbert is not At Home.

MARY: Then I shall wait for her. When will she be back?

MAIDSERVANT: I'm afraid you don't understand. Mrs Herbert is not seeing anyone.

MARY: Then I shall wait until she is.

MAIDSERVANT: You must do as you please but I warn you Mrs Herbert will not be At Home today.

MARY: I shall wait.

MAIDSERVANT: May I know your name?

MARY: Mrs Mary Seacole. I am an experienced nurse and doctoress. I have come to offer my services for the Crimea. Would you please tell Mrs Herbert my name and my errand? Here is a testimonial from the Medical Officer of the West Granada Mining Company.

The maid moves away and whispers to the footman. She takes the paper and moves across to Mrs. Stanley, and gives it to her. The footman looks Mary Seacole up and down insolently and turns away.

MRS STANLEY: *(Reading)* 'I became acquainted with Mrs Seacole... on the Isthmus of Panama and have had many opportunities of witnessing her professional zeal and ability in the treatment of tropical diseases... I am myself personally indebted for her kindness and skill... Her fitness for the duties of medical attendant needs no comment.'

MAIDSERVANT: She is a - very strange person, madam. She will not leave. She says she will wait until you can see her.

MRS HERBERT: Dear me.

She rises and holds out her hand to Miss Jelkes, who also rises.

I think we can offer you the opportunity to join Miss Nightingale. I am sure you are just what she is looking for. I hope you have a pleasant journey. Thank you for your splendid offer of help. You will be able to arrange the details of your passage to Scutari with Mrs Stanley.

MISS JELKES: Thank you, Mrs Herbert. I may be very inexperienced but I mean to become one of Miss Nightingale's best nurses. Thank you for this opportunity.

MRS HERBERT: It is our pleasure. (*To the maidservant*) Show Miss Jelkes out.

MAIDSERVANT: Yes ma'am.

She moves towards the door with Miss Jelkes. They stop by Mary and freeze.

MRS HERBERT: And what about this persistent Mrs Seacole?

MRS STANLEY: Persistent - yes. But she's -

She stops.

MRS HERBERT: Yes?

MRS STANLEY: She's - not the kind of woman we're looking for.

MRS HERBERT: In spite of these excellent testimonials?

MRS STANLEY: I don't think she would fit in. She might be a disruptive element. I hardly think Miss Nightingale will have much time for - native medicine.

MRS HERBERT: Then you had better tell her that we have all the nurses that we need.

MRS STANLEY: We are seeing some more candidates tomorrow.

MRS HERBERT: Then we must hope that Mrs Seacole doesn't come back tomorrow.

They freeze. Miss Jelkes looks curiously at Mary.

MARY: Excuse me. But have you been to see Mrs Herbert.

MISS JELKES: (*Coldly*) Yes. I have.

MARY: Do you hope to become one of Miss Nightingale's nurses?

MISS JELKES: I am one of Miss Nightingale's nurses.

MARY: Oh! Indeed! What is your particular skill? Are you very experienced in these matters? I have nursed a great many cholera victims. I have cured most of them. I have many skills to offer.

MISS JELKES: How interesting. Do excuse me. Good morning.

She goes out. Mary Stanley comes across to Mary Seacole.

MRS STANLEY: Mrs Seacole? Thank you so much for your kind offer. I am afraid we have our full complement of nurses -

MARY: Aren't you seeing any more women? What about tomorrow?

MRS STANLEY: No, Mrs Seacole, I repeat. We have all the nurses we need. There is no point in your waiting here. Mrs Herbert will not see you. You are wasting your time. Good morning.

She and Mrs Herbert return to their places. Mary turns centre stage and falls down on her knees. The cast move past her with curious glances.

MARY: (*Voice Over*) 'Did these ladies shrink from accepting my aid because my blood flowed beneath a somewhat duskier skin than theirs? Tears streamed down my foolish cheeks, as I stood in the fast thinning streets: tears of grief that Heaven should deny me the opportunity that I sought. Then I stood still and looking upward through the dark clouds that shadowed London, prayed aloud for help.'

Mary gets to her feet.

MARY: I don't care what happens. I am going to the Crimea!

She goes off upstage and sits at her desk, pen in hand.

Military music. The distant rumble of cannon. Neighing of horses. We are on Cathcart Hill. A war artist is looking out over the valley, and sketching what he sees. A maidservant brings in a camp-stool and her lady sits and looks through a little telescope. Another lady enters with a card in her hand. She is followed by a young pregnant woman. She moves across to the first lady but before she can speak Dr. Barry enters and goes to speak to the artist.

FIRST LADY: Dr. Barry!

DR. BARRY: (*Looking round impatiently*): Good morning, your Ladyship.

FIRST LADY: And what are you doing up on Cathcart Hill at this time of day?

DR. BARRY: Bursting with impatience, ma'am.

FIRST LADY: Dear me! How uncomfortable. Then you must come and explain to me what I am looking at.

Dr. Barry moves across and takes the telescope.

DR. BARRY: (*Brusquely*) Those are the Russian guns. Over there on the Heights. At the head of the Valley. Our quarters are down there. Our guns are drawn up there. The Heavy Brigade will be down there on the right.

FIRST LADY: all seems very confusing. I don't think I can see anything very clearly. I shall wait till the battle begins and I can pick out the colours. Why are you so impatient, Dr. Barry?

DR. BARRY: I beg your pardon, ma'am. That was rude of me. It would be better to say I am bursting with fury. I have nothing to do. I'm only here as Lord Raglan's guest. I'm not allowed to practise my medicine. I am forbidden to set foot on the wards - in spite of all my experience. Apparently I'm too old and too highly qualified to do any doctoring here.

FIRST LADY: Dear me. So why are you here?

DR. BARRY: Taken three months leave from Corfu. I'm going to kidnap as many of the wounded as I can and take them back to Corfu to recover.

FIRST LADY: You'd better start with this child's husband. One of Lord Cardigan's officers. Shot in the leg. Oh don't start crying, child. He's going to be all right. (*To Dr. Barry*) And as you can see she's in a delicate condition herself.

YOUNG WIFE: Oh Milady, I wish I'd never come to this dreadful place. Robert is hurt and they won't let me near him -

DR. BARRY: What the Nightingale woman and her dragons?

YOUNG WIFE: - and the flies and the noise and -

DR. BARRY: Pooh! That's nothing yet. Wait till our guns get going. You're right though. You get yourself back home. This is no place for women. Send 'em all back home I say.

SECOND LADY: But they're still coming out here. What do you think of this. Is this some kind of madwoman do you think? Look what's arrived. There are dozens of these cards.

DR. BARRY: (*Taking the card*) 'BRITISH HOTEL. Mrs Mary Seacole (late of Kingston Jamaica) respectfully announces to her former kind friends and to the Officers of the Army and Navy generally, that she has taken her passage in the screw-steamer 'Hollander' to start from London on the 25th of January, intending on her arrival at Balaclava to establish a mess-table and comfortable quarters for sick and convalescent officers.' Mad completely mad!

FIRST LADY: Exactly. It's only her card that arrived here. I don't suppose we'll see the woman herself.

They return to their places. A man lies groaning, near the beds. A nurse attempts to give him some water. Florence Nightingale enters.

FLORENCE NIGHTINGALE: Nurse. What do you think you are doing?

NURSE: Looking after this soldier, Miss Nightingale. He - was thirsty...

FLORENCE NIGHTINGALE: Who gave you permission to leave the ward?

NURSE: No-one, Miss Nightingale. He was crying out... Groaning... I came out to see what I could do.

FLORENCE NIGHTINGALE: Leaving the forty patients you were supposed to be looking after, unattended.

NURSE: No... Yes... I - they were quite calm. And he was crying so much. He's badly hurt.

FLORENCE NIGHTINGALE: He is not your responsibility. You have abandoned your responsibility. I will not have disobedience. You will return to your duties at once and tomorrow you will make arrangements to return to England.

NURSE: Miss Nightingale. Please. Let me stay. I didn't mean -

FLORENCE NIGHTINGALE: To England. I have no room for anyone who disobeys my orders. Back to your duty, Nurse.

NURSE: (*Snivelling, near to tears*) Yes, Miss Nightingale.

FLORENCE NIGHTINGALE: My nurses do not cry.

The nurse goes off. Florence Nightingale tends to the man. Mary Seacole crosses to meet Mrs Bracebridge.

MARY: Mrs Bracebridge?

MRS BRACEBRIDGE: Yes? Who on earth are you?

MARY: Mrs Mary Seacole. I have a letter from Dr. Forde for Miss Nightingale. (*Handing the letter to Mrs Bracebridge*)

MRS BRACEBRIDGE: And why have you come here, Mrs Seacole?

MARY: To be of use.

MRS BRACEBRIDGE: Oh but Miss Nightingale has the entire management of our hospital staff and I do not think that any vacancy -

MARY: Excuse me. ma'am, but I am bound for the front in a few days.

MRS BRACEBRIDGE: Indeed! Wait here for a few moments if you will be so good.

She crosses and gives the letter to Florence Nightingale, who moves downstage to greet Mary.

FLORENCE NIGHTINGALE: What is it that you want, Mrs Seacole - is there anything that we can do for you? If it lies in my power I shall be very happy.

MARY: All I need is a bed for the night and then tomorrow I can go up to the front and begin my task.

FLORENCE NIGHTINGALE: That is easily arranged. And I wish you well in your task

Florence Nightingale and Mary shake hands. Mary moves downstage and Florence back upstage. Little Mary moves forward with Sarah and Emily. Sarah scrubs the floor, Emily carries a washing basket full of clean clothes.

MARY: That's it, Sarah. I want that floor so clean you could eat off it. Is that my clean laundry, Emily?

EMILY: Yes, Mother Seacole.

MARY: Have you found any more handkerchiefs?

EMILY: No. There's not a handkerchief to be had.

MARY: No more old sheets to tear up?

EMILY: (*Shaking her head, sadly*) No, Mother Seacole.

MARY: My boys are desperate for clean hankies. We'll have to find something. (*Scratching herself vigorously*) Drat these fleas. They're as big as bluebottles. I swear they're a bigger pest than the Russians. Mary. Have you checked the stores? Coffee, tea, bacon, eggs. sausages Plenty of cakes? Don't you let any of those Turkish rascals alone in the stores. Those confounded wide trousers of theirs. They could get a full grown baby - or a pound of sausages - inside them.

LITTLE MARY: (*Giggling*) One of them the other day had tied his ankles tight and he'd pushed pounds of tea and coffee down his trousers. The officers cut the cords and held him up and shook out all the tea and coffee.

SARAH: I don't mind the fleas or the thieving Zouaves, it's the rats. A great big one - big as a cat - bit Francis the Cook's finger to the bone.

EMILY: And they nibbled his head. Where his hair was thin.

LITTLE MARY: And one great big huge one got into the picnic basket we made for the young gentleman and ate its way through all the pies and sausages.

SARAH: Worse than the Russians they are.

MARY: No. The thieves. The rats. The fleas. The mud. They're nothing. Nothing to what these poor, poor boys suffer. It's our job to give them the comfort they need. A wounded boy with his leg shot away will find the will to get better if he sees a friendly face, reminding him of home. What a shout there is when I go to the door of my caboose and call out 'Rice pudding day, my sons!' And there's no army more partial to pastry than the British army before Sebastopol. I've a reputation for sponge cakes that any pastry cook in London would be proud of. I dress their wounds, I cure their ills and I feed them, and cheer them along. My British Hotel is much more than a hospital.

Distant gunfire. Mary moves back to her desk, and stands

beside it. The women with her freeze. The Nurse kneels down and begins to scrub the floor between the beds. Florence Nightingale moves downstage to Dr. Barry.

DR. BARRY: Are you Miss Nightingale?

FLORENCE NIGHTINGALE: Yes, sir.

DR. BARRY: What on earth is going on here? What is being done to protect the water supply? Have you seen the state of those open drains?

FLORENCE NIGHTINGALE: Sir -

DR. BARRY: And what are your useless nurses doing cleaning? You could employ local cleaners for that.

FLORENCE NIGHTINGALE: Excuse me -

DR. BARRY: And then your nurses could get on with the job of nursing. Meanwhile you can give some of your patients to me. I'll take 'em back to Corfu with me.

FLORENCE NIGHTINGALE: Any number would help. I have hundreds.

DR. BARRY: Then I'll take hundreds. I'll guarantee to get them well.

Mary, Florence Nightingale and Dr. Barry all stand quite still downstage in separate pools of light.

FLORENCE NIGHTINGALE: I later learned that this bad-tempered doctor was a woman. Dr. James Barry, who was too highly qualified and distinguished a doctor to be allowed to walk the wards in the Crimea, died in 1865. And they discovered that 'he' was a woman who had had a child.

DR. BARRY: They wouldn't allow women to train as doctors. That was my ambition. Not a nurse but a doctor. And so I became a 'man'. and trained as a doctor in Edinburgh. The youngest to qualify - and the first female, though they didn't know that! I was an Army doctor all my life and I rose to the heights of my profession. And they never knew. They jeered at me for being effeminate. But of course I couldn't possible be female, could I? I was doing a man's job - and doing it better than they were. I had no patience with Miss Nightingale's feminine wiles.

FLORENCE NIGHTINGALE: When you hear of the Crimean War mine is the name that you think of first. Can you remember the names of the generals or the politicians or the doctors? I fought them all and I trained a disciplined band of women who were proud to call themselves Nurses. But I have no patience with foolish women who claim to be the equal of men and try to compete with them.

MARY: Have you ever heard my name? I went to the Crimea on my own, because no-one wanted the skills of a Creole woman from Jamaica. I came back poverty-stricken, my health destroyed. But my sons, the common soldiers and their officers, set up a fund for their old Mother Seacole. The nobility, royalty itself, were proud to be my friends. I was one of the most famous women in England. The doors that had been closed to me were suddenly open. I have no patience with those who despised my skills because of the colour of my skin. Perhaps, one day, people like me will be welcome as doctors - and nurses...

FIRST WOMAN: Mary Seacole died in 1881.

SECOND WOMAN: A memorial service was held on 14th May 1981.

THIRD WOMAN: The sick and the sorry can tell the story
Of her nursing and dosing deeds,
Regimental MD never worked as she
In helping sick men's needs.

FOURTH WOMAN: She gave her aid to all who prayed
To hungry and sick and cold
Open hand and heart, alike ready to part
Kind words and acts and gold.

TOGETHER: Still she'd take her stand, as blithe and bland.
With her stores, and jolly old soul -
And - be the right man in the place who can -
The right woman was Dame Seacole.

Music. Triumphant and cheerful.

THE END

THE STRAWBERRY TEA

CHARACTERS

RACHEL

SALLY

LIZ

GAVIN

PETER

The play is set in the library of a large modern school in the 1990s.

THE STRAWBERRY TEA

We are in the school library, an airy, peaceful, well-equipped room with pine shelves and furniture. One large, elegant, wooden table has been carefully set out for tea with delicate china cups and saucers, a big silver teapot, and small plates of cakes and biscuits.

At a second table, covered with a large plastic cloth, Rachel is busy making brown bread and cucumber sandwiches.

Sally is sitting watching her. She is comfortably curled up in one of the library's easy chairs. She has a notebook on her knee and a pen in her hand. She is using neither of them at the moment.

RACHEL: Oh this is useless! This butter's too hard and the bread's too thin. It's just tearing to pieces.

SALLY: Should have used the soft spread.

RACHEL: Don't be stupid. We can't give them margarine! Do you think I should cut the crusts off?

Sally grins in a deliberately infuriating manner.

SALLY: I dunno. Is it a bit naff because it's genteel to cut them off, or because it's common to leave them on? It might look as if we didn't know you cut the crusts off in the best circles. Or it might look as if we were trying to be posh and it isn't really. Like fish-knives. What do you reckon the Queen does?

RACHEL: Well, shall I or shan't I?

SALLY: Please yourself. Have you thought about doilies?

RACHEL: Oh shut up! Fat lot of use you are.

SALLY: We aim to please.

Liz enters, carrying a kettle.

LIZ: There is an electric point in here somewhere, isn't there?

RACHEL: Oh you can't bring the kettles in here. Keep them in the Home Economics Room.

LIZ: Don't be daft! That's ridiculous! Am I supposed to go running backwards and forwards with teapots all afternoon? The tea'll be stone cold.

RACHEL: Well, it doesn't look very nice having kettles in here.

SALLY: You could always borrow the urn!

RACHEL: No. We are not having that horrible thing in here. It's not a greasy spoon caff...

LIZ: Then you'll have to have the kettles.

RACHEL: Oh. It does spoil it...

SALLY: Why? After forty-five years of teaching, I think even Miss Allenbury has sussed out that you have to boil a few kettles to get a cup of tea. Indian or Chayna? Milk or lemon? Or should it be cream?

RACHEL: Oh shut up, Sally. If you're not going to do anything useful you can go.

SALLY: I am being useful. I'm working out my little speech. I can't be expected to do the catering as well.

LIZ: Look this plug here's all right. I don't care what you say, I'm bringing the kettles in here. I mean, it's in the corner. If you sit her at this end of the table she won't even see them.

RACHEL: Oh all right. It makes it all a bit make-shift though.

SALLY: Oh for goodness' sake calm down, Rachel. It is make-shift. This is the school library not the Ritz. Just the place for a really wild party.

RACHEL: I thought it would be the best place because it's near Home Economics and we could wheel things along on trolleys.

LIZ: Oh come on! Do you want us all in caps and aprons? This is all getting out of hand.

SALLY: Why don't we have it in Home Economics anyway?

RACHEL: Oh no - that'd be horrible. It'd be like an exam.

SALLY: Or the Sixth Form Common Room? She could read the graffiti while she was waiting for the kettle to boil.

RACHEL: No. The library's more suitable. More traditional...

SALLY: Oh gawd!

RACHEL: You needn't laugh -

SALLY: Miss A's not the only one coming, is she? The Common Room's always been good enough for the old ducks. This is the big wide world, you know. If you want to be traditional here give her a plastic bag and a can of paint-stripper.

RACHEL: Oh stop trying to be clever. She is the - well - the guest of honour. We've got to make a special effort...

SALLY: Tell that to the others.

RACHEL: Oh, you know what I mean. She's the one that's -

SALLY: Yes?

RACHEL: Well. Done something.

SALLY: And the others haven't?

RACHEL: Well. I suppose in their way. But they're only old ladies from the Hospice. Not like Miss - (*Defensively*) I don't suppose they've ever done anything much.

LIZ: How do you know? One old lady last year. Ever such an ordinary looking old lady. She'd been something quite high up - in secret operations in the War.

RACHEL: Oh Liz! You don't want to believe the tales they tell you. One old dear told me she was the one the Duke of Windsor really wanted to marry and Mrs Simpson'd kidnapped him to get him away from her. Half of 'em don't know what day it is.

SALLY: The other half do though! Hey! Perhaps Miss Allenbury made it all up. Perhaps she never set foot in a class-room in her life! Never taught anybody anything!

RACHEL: Don't be silly. She was a wonderful teacher, they say. A real inspiration to everybody.

> *Sally mimes playing a violin and hums* **Hearts And Flowers**. *Rachel flings down her knife.*

RACHEL: Oh! I hate this! I wish I didn't have to do it all.

SALLY: Come on. Don't get your knickers in a twist. We only got you to arrange it all because you're the best.

RACHEL: I know. That's what I hate. I hate organizing things.

LIZ: But you do it better than anybody else.

RACHEL: I know. And you all wind me up... Why can't I be useless like - well... When my exams are over I'm going to change. Just you wait. I'll be completely different. I won't do any homework and I won't turn up to any lessons and when people ask me to do things I'll say 'Nah, can't be bothered. Too much hassle.' And I won't be organized at all. And I'll leave and hitch round Europe.

SALLY: No you won't. After your exams - which you will pass with flying colours because you never stop working - you will be Head Girl and you will get a medal for Being Truly Wonderful All the Time. You're just a natural Girl Guide. I bet you were organized in your pram. I bet you had all your rattles and cuddly toys all lined up in alphabetical order, didn't you?

RACHEL: You don't like me, do you?

SALLY: No! I'm just your best friend, remember? Only you got us all into this mess. You've got to organize us all out of it again at the other side.

RACHEL: It's not supposed to be a mess!

The door opens and Gavin enters with a flourish bearing a tray of iced sponge cakes high above his head.

GAVIN: Ta Ra!!!!

RACHEL: Careful! Don't drop them!

Gavin puts them on the table

RACHEL: Hey! They're really good!

GAVIN: Of course they are. They are actually brilliant. If you want cakes made properly get the boys to do it. Who are all the Master chefs? The Master race! Us.

RACHEL: Oh yeah?

GAVIN: Yeah! You girls would have made perfectly eatable, workaday cakes. These are little artistic gems. Pete's bringing the biscuits. They're pretty good but not as good as mine.

SALLY: I think the nicest thing about you is your modesty, Gavin.

GAVIN: Yes. If anything I tend to understate my own brilliance.

RACHEL: There how does that look?

SALLY: (*Getting up to look at the table*) Fine. (*Drily*) We've only got an hour and a half to kick off. You'd better cover everything with cling-film or it'll all go dried up. Can't hand round curly cucumber sandwiches can we?

Rachel makes a little worried sound.

No it looks really great. Honestly. The old ducks'll love it.

LIZ: (*Joining them*) That's what you think. I reckon they'll all moan their heads off 'cos it's different this year. They moan enough anyway. There was one old bat last year - in a wheelchair. She never stopped. I gave her a tomato sandwich. She couldn't eat that because of the pips. Cheese gave her nightmares and cucumber repeated on her. She ate about seven sponge fingers and didn't leave any for anybody else on her table. She said that strawberries were too acid and we shouldn't give them acidy things. I said we always did a Strawberry Tea in June and she said it was a waste of money. Then she said she couldn't see anything and she was too close to the piano and it was dinning in her ears. I spent the whole afternoon wheeling her from plate to plate while she grabbed everything she could lay her hands on. Then at the finish she said it was about time we did something like this because youngsters today haven't got any manners and never think of anybody but themselves... Some of them were quite sweet though.

RACHEL: Well - I mean - oh dear! They won't be awkward this time will they? They will know it's Miss Allenbury's eightieth birthday as well.

GAVIN: That'll probably make matters worse. Some of them are over eighty. I reckon they'll throw a tantrum -

RACHEL: Oh no! I said right from the start it was an awful idea. We should have kept them separate. Given the O.A.Ps their Strawberry Tea and had another party for Miss Allenbury.

LIZ: Oh come on! We couldn't go through this twice. For goodness sake let's get it over in one!

GAVIN: Kill all the old birds with one stone.

LIZ: Or one of your rock cakes!

SALLY: I think you might find a bit - of a culture clash, Miss Allenbury remembering the dear old days when this was a Grammar School and everybody wore uniform and didn't speak in the corridors...

GAVIN: - and all the old biddies from the Home who want to play Bingo and sing **Just a Song at Twilight**. Great!!

RACHEL: Well it's not my fault. Mrs Terry said we had to have a party for Miss Allenbury. She's kept in touch all these years and always comes to everything and - gives donations and - that sort of thing.

LIZ: Haunts the place you mean.

SALLY: And the teachers who can remember her, can't stand her and the others can't be bothered and they've loaded it off onto us!

GAVIN: Have you thought how you're going to get the old ducks up here?

RACHEL: What do you mean?

GAVIN: Those three steps by the door.

SALLY: Hmm. (*Pause*) Well. We've still got time to shift all this down to the Sixth Form Common Room...

LIZ: Oh no! It's too late.

RACHEL: They're only little steps -

GAVIN: Little steps stop wheelchairs.

RACHEL: They're not all in wheelchairs. You boys will have to lift them up the steps.

GAVIN: Great!

RACHEL: I wish we could have had the Hall.

SALLY: Even Mrs Terry wouldn't shift a Maths exam for dear Miss Allenbury.

GAVIN: Well if me and Pete and Philip have to cart them all up the stairs, I reckon that lets us out of talking to them.

RACHEL: Oh no it doesn't. Come on Liz, Let's go and look at the steps. We could put a board over them perhaps. Let's go to the office and ask Mrs Morton how many of them are in wheelchairs.

GAVIN: Should have thought of that before.

RACHEL: Oh shut up! You all leave everything to me, don't you? Somebody could have thought of this sooner. Mrs Terry could have said!

LIZ: I wish it was seven o'clock tonight.

RACHEL: So do I!

They go out.

GAVIN: Rachel's going to explode one of these days.

SALLY: She likes to make a drama out of everything. If she's not worrying she worries.

Gavin takes a cake and eats it.

GAVIN: Well, it'll all be over in a couple of hours.

SALLY: Rachel will have counted those you know.

GAVIN: It's all right. I've re-arranged them, so she won't notice.

SALLY: Give me one.

GAVIN: Er. No. I can't re-arrange them that much. Have a sandwich.

SALLY: No thanks...

She looks round the table and eventually picks up a biscuit.

SALLY: At least you don't have to make a speech.

GAVIN: It's your own fault. You shouldn't be so brilliant at English.

SALLY: It's not that. I would have got out of it if it was just that. Miss A. taught my Mum and she volunteered me for it.

GAVIN: You should have said no.

SALLY: You don't say no to my Mum. Not if you want to get out with your ears intact.

GAVIN: Yeah?

SALLY: It's easier to do what she says. She only goes on if you don't. She'd come into my room at midnight and sit on the bed and say, 'Sally. darling. Have you really thought about this? I don't want to interfere but - I must say I'm disappointed in you. I thought you had more of a sense of responsibility blah blah blah.' And she goes on and on and accuses me of being sullen and says I was such a sunny little girl she doesn't know what's gone wrong.

GAVIN: I wouldn't put up with it.

SALLY: Well, I'll be leaving home soon. She wants me to go to London University because she did and I can live at home and tell her everything just like sisters!... I've put Aberdeen for my first choice. She doesn't know that.. I filled my UCCA form in pencil at home and then changed it. If there was a University of the Outer Hebrides that did English and Philosophy I'd go there.

GAVIN: My Mum's given up on me. Spends all her time worrying about Jake.

SALLY: I'm not surprised. He's mad.

GAVIN: Yeah. He's suspended again.

SALLY: How long for?

GAVIN: End of term. We haven't seen him since yesterday morning.

SALLY: Where's he gone?

GAVIN: Dunno. I think he's probably pinched a car and gone down to Eastbourne. He's got this mate there that wants to start a band. He'll finish up in gaol. The sooner the better. He's a real psychopath! Then perhaps my Mum can think about something else for a change. When I told her I was going to do Maths, Physics and Biology instead of History, Politics and French she said that'll be nice and did I think Jake was on drugs.

SALLY: You're not going to are you?

GAVIN: Don't be stupid. I was just testing... I think I'll strip naked, this afternoon, paint myself blue, rush in here and throw trifles at all the old ladies.

SALLY: They might like that.

GAVIN: People only bother about you if you cause trouble.

SALLY: You're joking! If you get caught up with somebody like my mother she'll bully you whatever you do. I just sit around and say, 'Yes Mummy.' all the time. Doesn't make a bit of difference. And she still can't work out why Dad's shacked up with this dimbo who makes two short planks look like **University Challenge**.

GAVIN: Perhaps we could swap.

SALLY: The worst bit is - she's coming this afternoon.

GAVIN: No! God! -

SALLY: Yes. I begged her not to. But she went to Mrs Terry. 'Miss Allenbury did everything for me... and Sally's doing the speech... I know it's not usual but could I just slip in at the back?' La Terry just caved in. Got no choice!

GAVIN: I'll go and talk to your Mum then. All about you!

SALLY: You dare!

GAVIN: I'm not going around chatting up all the geriatrics. I can't talk to old people. I never know what to say. You girls amaze me... Rabbiting on like you've known them all your life.

SALLY: That's what girls are supposed to do, isn't it? You'll be all right. They'll all think you're a lovely-looking boy. And they'll ask you which is your girl-friend and say, 'Isn't she lucky!' and they'll keep saying to us, 'Isn't it good of all the boys to come along when they could be playing football?' They'll just expect us to be there!

GAVIN: In that case I want an announcement that I made the cakes. And I'll take a bow. You can put that in as part of your speech.

SALLY: God knows what I'm going to say! I mean, I never knew her and from what Mum says she was a terrible old bat. One of the real old-fashioned sort... 'You could do with a few more teachers like that nowadays instead of all these trendy scruffs that seem to teach you... I can't tell which are the teachers sometimes!!'

> *Gavin grins in assent. They are both silent for a moment. Sally goes back to her chair and looks at her notes. Dubiously, she scribbles a few lines then crosses them out ferociously. Gavin watches her.*

SALLY: He is, I suppose? Jake I mean.

GAVIN: Probably. Couldn't give a toss.

Sally tears up her notes and scatters them in the air.

GAVIN: You'll cop it when Rachel gets back.

He bends down and picks up a piece of paper.

Hey! There's nothing on this bit.

SALLY: There's nothing on any of it. I'm going to make it up as I go along.

She gets to her feet. Clears her throat theatrically and begins.

SALLY: We are here to pay tribute to Miss Allenbury who is eighty today and first came to this school in Boadicea's time. For thirty years she ruled this school with a rod of iron and scared everybody witless. She saw off five Headmistresses and thousands of girls. If she didn't drive them to Oxford or Cambridge, she drove them stark raving mad. She only left when they turned the place from a lovely, cosy Grammar School into a low, vulgar Comprehensive and let in... boys! She is a pathetic old thing, today, because, for fifteen years, since she retired she hasn't had anything to do, so she keeps coming here and tut-tutting about all the changes, and getting on everybody's nerves. We're giving her a little party today in the hope she'll take the hint. She doesn't like boys and she doesn't think they're at all necessary, and she's not mad about girls now. We couldn't face the thought of having her here on her own, so we've tacked her onto the OAPs' Summer Tea. They don't know who she is and she wouldn't want to know them. We, the Lower Sixth, have organized this terrible afternoon because we couldn't get out of it. We will now sing **Lead Kindly Light amid the encircling Gloom**, and look in our Lucky Dip bags.

GAVIN: That ought to do nicely.

Peter comes in with a guitar and prowls round the room.

PETER: Where's Rachel?

SALLY: Gone to the Office. She'll be back in a minute.

PETER: (*Hardly listening*) Oh Good. There's loads of points in here.

SALLY: We need them for the kettles. Anyway she'll never let you play your electric guitar. You've got to play **Scarborough Fair** on that one and like it.

PETER: It would have been much better in the Hall with Mrs Aylott on the piano.

SALLY: Yes. We know that.

PETER: They're bound to want to sing things I've never heard of.

GAVIN: You'll be all right. Just play a couple of chords and say 'All together now!' and they'll fill in the rest.

PETER: I don't know any of the things they'll want to sing. Can't we get the piano in here? Mrs Aylott can play anything -

SALLY: The old ladies'll like you better. Any kind action performed by a boy is worth three by a mere female. Anyway you are not getting out of anything!

GAVIN: Do you know **When I'm Sixty-Four**?

SALLY: That's teenage rubbish for this lot. You'll have 'em all in tears for their lost youth. I tell you what. When I'm eighty, I'm not going to sit around singing **Knees up Mother Brown**... My Gran won't go to any of these things. She says she's always liked walking in the Lake District and string quartets and why should people assume she likes Bingo just because she's seventy-two?

GAVIN: I bet Miss Allenbury won't play Bingo either.

PETER: When's Rachel coming back? I want to know what I'm supposed to be doing. Otherwise I'm just going home and stuff the old folks.

SALLY: Oh no, you're not!! You're going to stay here and suffer with the rest of us.

Rachel and Liz come back, looking rather shaken.

SALLY: Oh there you are. About time. You've got a near mutiny on your hands. Pete wants to slope off -

She looks at Rachel properly for the first time.

What's up?

RACHEL: We went to the Office... Mrs Terry was there... Miss Allenbury's had a stroke. Her niece found her when she went round this morning... to help her to - get ready. They took her to hospital but she was dead when they got there. They've just 'phoned the Office - her niece, Mrs Morton, was on the 'phone when me and Liz got there... Mrs Terry's getting the book and the picture... I suppose she'll give them to the niece.

There is a long pause.

GAVIN: What's going to happen then?

RACHEL: I don't know. Mrs Terry'll be along in a minute.

LIZ: (*Slowly*) We can't cancel it - they'll all be on their way here.

GAVIN: What'll we say to them all?

SALLY: Nothing. They didn't know her.

PETER: You can't do that. They know it was going to be different this afternoon.

SALLY: It's that all right.

RACHEL: We - I suppose - we'll just have to tell them.

SALLY: Great party! Hello. Come on in and enjoy yourselves. The guest of honour can't be here on account of she's just shuffled off this mortal coil. She was about your age, but don't let that spoil it for you.

RACHEL: Sally!

SALLY: Sorry.

LIZ: I don't suppose they'll bother much. They must be used to it.

PETER: Why?

LIZ: Well - at their age - I mean - it must be happening all the time.

GAVIN: Probably be glad it's not them.

Rachel wanders over to the table. Sally collects up the torn bits of paper she scattered earlier. Peter strums his guitar.

SALLY: Well. At least it lets me out of making a speech. Mrs Terry can do all the talking. I'm too young. What's she done with the book, did you say?

RACHEL: It's in the Art Room. Jackie was just finishing the inscription.

PETER: She'd better put **R.I.P** now, hadn't she?

LIZ: Pete!

Peter drags his fingers across the strings of the guitar.

SALLY: It was a good choice. The book... (*Her voice trails away*) I might as well 'phone Mum and put her off...

RACHEL: Oh I'm so depressed! It was going to be so good!

The others look round ruefully at the feast.

LIZ: When should I put the kettles on, do you think?

They all remain quite still as lights fade.

THE END

FLATMATES

CHARACTERS

STEVE

LYNN

TOM

TONY

CORALIE

The play is set in a student flat in the 1990s.

FLATMATES

We are in the sitting room of a large basement flat in an old Georgian house. It is fairly sparsely furnished with a couple of battered old armchairs, two or three dining chairs, a low coffee table and two rough bookshelves, crammed with books. Just right of centre is a large wooden dining table. There is no table cloth on it, and it is loaded with milk bottles, juice cartons, cereal packets, sliced bread, cotton-wool balls etc.

Steve, a lazy looking young man of about twenty, has cleared a space for himself and is eating a large breakfast. Lynn (aged nineteen) is sitting opposite him, removing her nail varnish.

STEVE: (*Irritably*) Do you have to do that here, Lynn? It's an appalling stink. Puts me off my breakfast.

LYNN: (*Calmly continuing with her nails*) Steve. A nuclear explosion wouldn't put you off your food.

STEVE: Well, a little consideration wouldn't come amiss. What do you want to paint your bloody fingernails at this hour for anyway?

LYNN: (*Lightly*) Pompous prat!

She has a cotton wool ball soaked in nail varnish remover in her hand.

Anyway I'm taking it off not putting it on.

She smiles sweetly at him and drops the cotton wool ball into his coffee cup. Steve removes it with an expression of distaste and holds it at arm's length.

STEVE: Lynn. For God's sake! Don't be so stupid. Look what you've done. Ruined a perfectly good cup of coffee!

LYNN: Sorry. I thought you'd finished. I'll make you another one.

STEVE: No thank you! I'm not drinking your instant muck. This happens to be a cup of decent coffee.

LYNN: Oh pardon me! Just give me time to shin up the Blue Mountains and pick a few beans to make you another cup.

STEVE: Don't be childish.

He gets up and goes out towards the exit to the kitchen up left. As he passes Lynn's chair he drops the coffee-soaked, remover-stained cotton wool into her lap.

Yours, I think.

LYNN: Owwww! That's my dressing gown if you don't mind!

STEVE: It's filthy already isn't it? Anyway, you should be properly dressed by now. Slut.

He goes out. Lynn puts her tongue out at him. She gets up, crosses to his side of the table and picks up a piece of bacon from his plate and eats it.

Tom comes in. He is fully dressed, looking rather crumpled, very pale and exhausted. Lynn looks at him dispassionately, as if this is exactly what she expected.

LYNN: God, you look awful.

Tom looks at her with a jaundiced eye.

TOM: Julia Roberts could just about get away with that dressing gown. You can't.

LYNN: Thank you kindly, Sir, she said.

TOM: Where's Steve?

LYNN: Gone to make himself another cup of gourmet coffee. I dunked a cotton wall ball in the one he was drinking.

TOM: Really, Lynn, you are childish.

Pause

LYNN: Why don't you go out and come back in again and pretend you like me.

TOM: I do like you. (*Pause*) But you irritate me.

LYNN: (*Drily*) The irritation is mutual.

Tom crosses to the table and rests his head on his arms on the table. Lynn looks at him ruefully.

LYNN: What time did you get to bed last night?

TOM: This morning... Five o' clock... I heard the dawn chorus.

LYNN: The only possible circumstances to hear the dawn chorus is after an all night party. Preferably on the river.

TOM: I had an essay.

LYNN: Haven't we all? When was it for? A fortnight's time?

TOM: Wednesday.

LYNN: (*Exasperated*) Then why stay up all night when you've got four days to do it in?

TOM: (*Almost to himself*) I've got it all worked out. I won't get it all done if I don't stick to this schedule. Get up at eight. Work till one. Take an hour off for lunch... Could read then I suppose... Work two till seven. Dinner. Then work through till three or four... Four hours' sleep is plenty...

LYNN: Then the men in white coats come and take you away to the funny farm.

Tom shakes his head, his eyes closed, as if he could shake away his thoughts and what Lynn is saying.

Tom! For goodness' sake, you'll have a breakdown. It's not what it's all about! You must ease up a bit.

TOM: It's all right for you. I can't afford to mess about like you. I've got so many things I want - It would be a disaster if I - Oh don't - don't lecture me, Lynn.

LYNN: (*Exasperated*) Oh you make me sick! I haven't done an essay for three weeks... The sky hasn't fallen in. I am still here. Dear old Freddie still turns up to my tutorials and waffles on about Eng. Lit. And what sort of rubbish are you churning out in the small hours, anyway? Come to terms with life, darling! All work and no play -

TOM: Oh shut up Lynn! I don't need advice from someone like you! I mean, it's difficult to believe in anyone as - flimsy - as you! Even your shallows have shallows.

LYNN: (*Quietly, a little hurt*) That's not even original. If I weren't such a radiantly lovely person I could take offence at you, you know. Have some breakfast. (*Pause*) OK. Suit yourself.

Tom stands absolutely still for a moment staring at the table. Lynn watches him intently. He looks round as if he

> *does not know where he is and closes his eyes. Lynn crosses to him and touches his cheek very briefly and looks at her finger tips.*

LYNN: (*Softly*) Don't cry, Tom.

TOM: (*Wincing*) I am not crying. That's sweat.

LYNN: Pouring out of your eyes? Tom...

TOM: No Lynn!

> *He turns away from her abruptly. Lynn shrugs and rather ostentatiously goes back to her fingernails. Tom crosses to the table and pours some cornflakes into a bowl. He looks round at the table and picks up a milk bottle with about an inch of milk in it.*

TOM: I do not believe it! Look at this!

LYNN: (*Flatly*) It's milk.

> *Tom crosses to the kitchen door. And yells offstage.*

TOM: Steve!!!! Steve!

> *Steve comes back with a cup of coffee, sees Tom with the milk bottle held towards him accusingly, takes it and pours it into his coffee. Tom is momentarily too taken aback to speak. Steve hands him back the empty bottle. And crosses and sits at the table again.*

STEVE: Cheers, old son.

TOM: Steve! You've taken my milk again! Look! I marked the bottle last night. Three quarters of it's gone. How dare you?!

STEVE: (*Equably*) Sorry. I needed it for my porridge.

TOM: Give me strength! Why couldn't you go down to the Deli. and get some of your own?

STEVE: Couldn't leave the flat, old son. My bacon would have caught fire.

LYNN: (*Drily*) He's managed his usual anorexic's breakfast. Porridge - sugar - cream - fruit-juice - kippers - bacon - eggs - tomato - beans - mushrooms - sausages - black pudding - liver - kidney - fried bread - toast - marmalade - coffee -

STEVE: - nail varnish remover -

LYNN: Just plugged the odd gap till elevenses at half past nine when he'll toy with a packet of choccy biccies and a litre of coffee!

TOM: If you touch my biscuits I'll murder you!

He speaks with a quiet intensity which surprises the others.

STEVE: Never eat charcoal biscuits, old son.

TOM: Very funny. Now you can go and buy me a pint of milk to make up for the one you stole. (*Shaking with anger, as Steve looks at him with a wry grin*) Go on!!

STEVE: Not now, old son, I'm drinking my coffee.

TOM: You've no right to steal my milk. We agreed - I can't afford milk every day - especially for you to slosh around when you feel like it!

Pause. Steve looks at Tom. Tom glares back at him. Slowly Steve pulls a fifty pence piece out of his pocket and flips it across at Tom. It falls on the floor.

STEVE: There you are. There's the money. Get yourself another bottle. Oh, and keep the change.

TOM: Steve, I am not joking.

STEVE: Could have fooled me.

He sits, legs stretched out in front of him, his hands behind his head. He grins at Tom, very relaxed and insolent.

TOM: Get up! And go and get me that pint of milk!!

LYNN: Oh use mine. I'll have my coffee black.

TOM: NO!! He's got to go and get me some milk.

STEVE: (*Quietly. Sweetly*) Don't say 'got to' to me, Tom.

TOM: (*Shaking*) Steve, I'm not standing for this.

STEVE: Sit down then. Or pick up that 50p and go and get some milk. Mustn't leave money lying around, old son. That could be all I had between me and starvation!

TOM: You'll never starve. As long as you go round stealing everybody else's food and milk, you - you conniving bastard!

LYNN: Tom! Cool it! You're tired. There's no need to be so nasty.

STEVE: No? I thought he couldn't help it.

Tom picks up the 50p coin and slams it down on the table.

TOM: There's your piece of silver. *(A wild, almost comic shriek)* Judas!!!

He rushes out. There is a pause.

STEVE: Tom is getting very tiresome, don't you think?

LYNN: He's not the only one.

STEVE: I don't like scenes.

LYNN: God! When I moved out of college to When I moved out of college to share with you lot I thought I was leaving all these tantrums behind! You're worse than Katie and Abby! At least they only rowed about who'd pinched whose fella! That I could cope with. But wheels within undercurrents are more than I can take!

She collects together all her manicure equipment and begins to shove them into the cotton wool bag.

STEVE: What a command of metaphor you do have, my dear Lynn. Strikes me all you English lot have got too much time on your hands and not enough intellectual meat... What was that you wrote - when you last wrote an essay that is - all that junk about the 'closely woven texture' of George Eliot's prose? Closely woven cerrap! It's unhealthy all this poring over literature. Makes you think you've got feelings. You all need a dose of nice, detached, unemotional law.

LYNN: And when did you last read any law?

STEVE: I don't need to. I just sit here and soak it up. *(Pushing away his plate)* Now. What shall I have for lunch? There's a rather piquant little terrine of crab I've had my eye on for a while. But do I feel fishy today? And would Tom cast it in my face in a rage thinking I'd been at his tinned pilchards?

LYNN: Look, Steve. Leave Tom alone. I'm worried about him. I think he's cracking up.

STEVE: That's his fault isn't it? If he must work so hard to please that rancid little mouse of a mother of his, that's his problem.

LYNN: Steve! What a spiteful thing to say!... His mother's rather pathetic...

STEVE: Exactly. She believes Tom is the sun, the moon and the stars for one thing.

LYNN: I think it's sweet. She's so proud of him.

STEVE: A bloodsucker. Keeping poor old Tom scribbling little pictures labelled 'Mummy' and writing pathetic letters from 'your loving little son'. It's time he shoved her under a bus and went out and did something outrageous like going on the Tube without paying! Much better to have a mother like mine. She can just about remember who I am when I'm actually there. She lost interest in me when I stopped being a curly headed little accessory to her fashion photos... Tom's wound up so tight there'll be bits found all over the Home Counties when he finally splits!

LYNN: I am a bit scared. I wouldn't know what to do if he really cracked up.

STEVE: Get out of the way! Don't be self-indulgent, Lynn. All you're really bothered about is a good time - so don't pretend to be all caring and compassionate about Tom. It's nauseating. Mummy'll come and pick up the pieces and put them in a plastic bag and take them home and stick them all together again. (*Pause*) I'm thinking of asking Tom to leave actually.

LYNN: Steve! You can't! He hasn't got a bean. It'd kill him if - he really would go right round the twist if he had to live on his own... Not that he could afford it.

STEVE: Are you suggesting that *we* keep him sane? He's only paying me half of what you do, you know. Why should I subsidise Tom because I've had the forethought to have a rich Mummy and Daddy who look after me instead of a whinging little apology of a female who managed to get herself pregnant at fifteen and didn't do anything about it. I think it's unhealthy to have a mother who's only a few years older than you. And who was his Dad? Some visually handicapped passer-by?

LYNN: Shut up! You're not supposed to know any of that, Don't you dare say anything!

STEVE: I never promise to keep secrets, Lynn dear. Much too exhausting.

LYNN: But I told you that in confidence.

STEVE: So?

LYNN: Look. I could afford a couple of quid more. Don't put Tom out.

STEVE: My dear! It's not the money. I don't want your grubby lucre. I just think I'm tired of Tom. Why this sudden interest in him, anyway? Are you after him?

LYNN: God no! I just -

STEVE: - feel sorry for him. Exactly.

Lynn turns away, biting her lip. Steve gets up, stretching.

STEVE: I'm off now. To select my lunch. One little thing I want you to do. As a founder member of our little flat-sharing co-operative. There's a girl called Coralie - yes! - coming at eleven to look over the flat.

LYNN: Why?

STEVE: To see if she'd like Tom's room.

LYNN: Steve. No!! Listen. Don't you go... It may be your flat but we agreed that we'd take all our decisions jointly. You can't put Tom out unless he agrees! You can't do this. I won't let you!

STEVE: Oh please don't get so worked up so early! We all agreed if you remember that we needed somebody else since Emily left us for 'fresh fields and pastures new' That's Milton, by the way. Heard of him?

LYNN: 'Fresh woods' is Milton. 'Fresh fields' is a common vulgar error.

STEVE: Been taking pomposity lessons from Tom, have we?... Be that as it may, we need another girl. You are a girl and the best person to decide about her. Now I come to think of it you were fast asleep on the floor when we discussed it. So. Coralie - a music student - is coming to give us the once-over... I may yet put Tom in the little backroom, though, then we could forget about him.

LYNN: We can't have a music student. What does she play?

STEVE: Who knows? Anyway, if she's as conscientious as you she'll never touch the thing. Probably spends all her time pushing those little black dots around in an artistic manner. But you do have a point. She might be better shut away in the back room. I'd like to humiliate Tom somehow, though. Difficult problem. Anyway, Coralie will be here in a few minutes. You can decide about her.

LYNN: I'm not doing it. You got her to come here -

STEVE: You can weed her out. If you think she's a possible, I can see her and give my casting vote. If not, we can set Tom on her and frighten her off. You could do the washing up while you're waiting. The table could do with a bit of a polish as well. I don't really like eating in all this squalor.

He shakes his head and goes out quickly.

LYNN: (*Shouting after him*) I'm not doing your dirty work for you! I am not interviewing this girl. I'm not. I mean it. Steve!!

There is a sudden loud ring at the doorbell. Steve pops his head back in at the door.

STEVE: Coralie?

LYNN: Or Tom forgot his key.

STEVE: I hope so. It's too early for Coralie. It's so rude being early for anything.

He goes out again and comes back with Coralie and Tony.

STEVE: Come in do. I'm afraid I've just got to go out for a while. I'm Steve. This is Lynn who makes all our decisions. Do make yourselves at home. I'll see you, Lynn. This is Coralie Mackintosh and er-

TONY: Tony Peel.

STEVE: Nice to meet you, Tony. 'Bye.

He disappears. Lynn is fuming.

LYNN: Ah. Well. Yes. Would you like to sit down?

Coralie sits at the table where Lynn was sitting earlier. Tony moves away and sits down, apparently taking no further interest in the proceedings. Coralie looks sourly at Lynn's nail paraphernalia on the table and pushes it aside. Lynn is too angry to be civil. She is very grudging and ungracious. Coralie is impervious to her manner.

LYNN: Oh. Sorry. That's my - rubbish.

CORALIE: (*Serenely*) I dislike the smell.

LYNN: Ah. (*Looking from one to the other*) Would you like some coffee?

Tony shakes his head.

CORALIE: I never touch caffeine.

Lynn pulls a face and casts her eyes, heavenwards. Coralie looks at the breakfast débris on the table.

That's a low-fibre cereal. You'd be much better off with a high-fibre one, and skimmed milk. - I'd like to bet that porridge was made with whole milk, instead of water, then drowned in sugar and cream. And that plate is running with animal fat. Whole oranges would be much better than all this juice. People think it's doing them good because there's no sugar in it. But it isn't you know. There's no fibre in it.

LYNN: That's not mine. It's the boys'.

CORALIE: Yes. I'm not surprised. It's very rare for the male of the species to have sensible ideas about food. Or exercise.

LYNN: (*Brightly*) I like champagne for breakfast myself. When I can get it.

CORALIE: Champagne - in moderation - is not an unhealthy drink.

LYNN: Good.

TONY: (*Belligerently*) What about this room then?

LYNN: Well. it's the room down the corridor. It looks out over the garden. Well up to the garden, actually. Basement flat - it doesn't get a lot of light but it's quite a - reasonable size. The bathroom's next door. You're a music student aren't you? What do you play?

CORALIE: Clarinet. I should need to play that here, but it isn't an unpleasant sound. And I do play it well. And piano. I don't have a piano. But that will not be a problem. I have an electronic keyboard

LYNN: Yes. Well. I don't think we'd be too disturbed by a clarinet. Lucky it wasn't drums. Or the double bass.

CORALIE: I do not play the drums. *(Pause)* Or the double bass. *(Pause)* Down the corridor you say. Tony! Go and look at the room. Oh. May Tony go and have a look?

LYNN: Yes. Of course. It's down the corridor...

Tony goes out.

LYNN: *(To herself)* One day I am going to kill Steve with my bare hands.

CORALIE: Steve is the person who showed me in?

LYNN: Yes.

CORALIE: And there's one other person here?

LYNN: Tom. Yes.

CORALIE: How long have you been sharing?

LYNN: Just this year. Me, that is. It's Steve's flat. Well, his parents'. He and Tom have been here two years. I was in college my first year and in a cupboard with alleged friends last year.

CORALIE: And what is - what are - the relationships between you?

Lynn is stunned.

LYNN: Me and Steve and Tom?

CORALIE: Yes.

LYNN: *(Angry)* I don't see it's any of your business.

CORALIE: It obviously affects whether I come here or not. I have a great deal of work to get through and I couldn't possibly live in an atmosphere of tensions and squabbles and upheavals. When people are 'living together', or 'having a relationship', I find it very unsettling. And I can't be disturbed in any way.

LYNN: We are flatmates. The room is only for one, you know. Were you intending to bring - Tim - with you?

CORALIE: Certainly not. Tony lives at home. He is, I suppose you might say, my boyfriend. Though I think that's a vulgar expression. He has a better eye for my practical needs than I have. Or he likes to think so. So he'll be able to tell me if this room will suit me. Actually I am quite capable of arranging the practical side of my life but I find the details boring.

LYNN: I see.

CORALIE: Tony is good at boring details.

After a moment Lynn realises that Coralie means this as a joke. She looks glumly at her feet. Coralie notices.

(*Coldly*) Is there any point in my staying?

LYNN: Why?

CORALIE: You seem quite determined to have nothing to do with me. If you are interviewing me on your flatmates' behalf shouldn't you ask me a few questions? Or, should I come back again when Steve and - er - Tom are here? Perhaps they might have more to say? Or do you really make all the decisions?

LYNN: I ought to say I'm sorry. But I'm not. Oh! Not you. I only heard about you a few minutes ago. Steve's little joke. He is a wealthy, spoilt brat who's only interested in his stomach. When he's not eating he pushes people around for fun. Tom is a raging neurotic with a chip on his shoulder, who is busy working himself into a really juicy breakdown. They fight. Incessantly. I spend as little time as possible here because both of them, in their different ways, cling to the sweet old-fashioned notion that - deep down - I am longing to do their washing and cooking for them, and I only refuse because I'm scared that the sisters' heavy mob will come and do me over if I give way to my natural instincts and start mothering them both. Steve is reading law - officially. Tom and I are both doing English. He always hands his work in on the dot. I don't even do the work. So tutorials are a permanent embarrassment specially as I'm brighter than he is. He tries to make me work - to fulfil my potential. I refuse. He manages to miss the point about absolutely everything. Life *and* Literature. And he is scared of girls. In case they don't measure up to Mummy. Steve's scared of them too. In case they don't take food seriously... If you think that's a calmer atmosphere than people 'having a relationship' as you call it - getting up at lunchtime, gazing into each other's eyes instead of lunch, then disappearing for the afternoon and going for long intense walks all evening - well, you're welcome to move in right now! Rent money in advance. Strict demarcation of the 'fridge. Steve has three quarters of it. The rest of us share the one remaining shelf. Gas meter. Immersion Heater. Telephone timer. Put your calls down in the book. Launderette down the road. Delicatessen and paper shop on the corner. No credit. The Dairy stopped delivering milk because we always managed to be out when he called to be paid. Or hid. Or didn't have the money in Tom's case. (*Pause*) Is that the sort of thing you were looking for?

CORALIE: Possibly. It depends on the room. I wouldn't involve myself in any way with any of you. I have far too much to do to worry about other people's little tantrums. You'd see very little of me. I don't know how much you'd hear, of course. Tony would not be allowed to come here except at certain weekends. He is a born-again Christian and has old-fashioned ideas about the relationship between the sexes, as well, and the rights and duties involved. But I drew up a list of conditions when we first met and he seems reasonably happy to adhere to them. Have you ever thought of doing that here? If you lead such messy lives

LYNN: (*Ruefully*) 'The best laid schemes o' mice and men gang aft agley'. You're Scottish aren't you?

CORALIE: Yes. But that doesn't mean I subscribe to the ideas of Robert Burns.

LYNN: I would have thought that was a harmless enough observation.

CORALIE: I don't believe in leaving things to chance. May I see this room? Tony's taking a long time.

LYNN: Yes. Of course. This way.

> *Coralie goes out, in front of Lynn who pulls a 'what have we here?' face, shrugs expressively, then follows her out, with a resigned air.*
>
> *After a moment Tom returns with a bottle of milk, and pours the milk onto his cornflakes. He then takes a Pentel from his pocket and marks the bottle. He takes a book from*

his other pocket and props it up against the milk bottle and begins to read and eat his cornflakes, occasionally making a mark in the book.

Tony returns. He has a notebook and pencil and is making notes. He sits in the armchair. After a moment Tom becomes aware that he is no longer alone and turns and glances curiously at Tony.

TONY: I'm with Coralie.

TOM: Oh.

TONY: She's looking at the room with - er - Lynn.

TOM: Oh. (*Pause*) Who's Coralie?

TONY: She's my girlfriend. She's a music student. Clarinet. She's come about the room.

TOM: Oh. Emily's room. Yes. I remember something. Vaguely. Are you moving in as well?

TONY: No. I live at home. No sense in wasting money when you've got a perfectly good base to work from. And I don't approve of co-habitation. On religious grounds.

TOM: Right... What are you reading?

TONY: I'm just making a few notes about the room... Oh. I see. No. I'm not a student. No time for that sort of nonsense. I work for an insurance broker. It's a very good job. Interesting as well. And good prospects. If you've got the right sort of initiative. What do you do?

TOM: I'm reading English.

TONY: That's a pretty useless sort of subject isn't it? What will you do with that? Teach? You'd have done better to do Maths or one of the Sciences. They're much more in demand.

TOM: I like literature.

TONY: Ah. Don't get me wrong. I read a bit myself. But I couldn't make a life of it. Like Coralie's music. Classical Music, that is. That's always seemed a bit pointless. I suppose it's not bad if you can get a good steady job in an orchestra. There's a lot of competition though. Doesn't seem like work to me. Never thought I'd finish up with a girlfriend who played the clarinet. It really means a lot to her as well, you know. Life's weird, isn't it?

TOM: Perhaps you won't finish up with her.

TONY: (*Coldly*) I think that's my business.

Tom looks at him thoughtfully.

TOM: Excuse me. I want to finish this.

He turns away and goes back to his book. Tony crosses and looks over his shoulder.

TONY: Poetry? Well. There you are.

He goes back to his armchair and gets on with his calculations as if he has just proved his point. A pause.

TONY: Whose is that big room - next to the kitchen?

TOM: Mine.

TONY: And those two inter-connecting rooms at the side?

TOM: Steve's.

TONY: And that leaves Lynn with the room at the front. I see.

Tom looks at him but does not answer. Steve comes in, carrying a large carrier bag.

STEVE: Ah. (*To Tony*) Is your name Coralie?

TONY: No. I'm Tony Peel. We met before. I'm Coralie's - unofficial fiancé.

STEVE: Steve Lansdowne. So we did. I was preoccupied. I hadn't decided about my lunch. And I am about to become Coralie's - unofficial landlord. I take it you've met Tom - our unofficial intellectual.

He puts the bag down and begins to unpack it lovingly.

There we are. Paté (*To Tom*) I decided against the crab. This is wild boar. I hope I haven't made a mistake. Smoked chicken. Quails' eggs. Balsamic vinegar. Walnut oil. Do you think Lynn would like to whip me up a bit of mayonnaise?

TOM: No.

STEVE: No. Nor do I. Pity. My arm gets so tired with all that beating. Olives. French bread. Unsalted butter. Endive. And a delicious white peach. That should keep me going till tea.

TONY: You'd better not let Coralie see that. She disapproves of unhealthy food.

STEVE: I wouldn't let Coralie touch a morsel of it. (*As Coralie and Lynn re-enter*) You don't want my wild boar paté, do you, Coralie?

CORALIE: Certainly not. It won't do you any good either.

STEVE: Good. I hate being done good to. Well, are you moving in with us?

LYNN: Steve -

Coralie crosses to the table, holding out her hand to Tom.

CORALIE: I'm Coralie Mackintosh. How do you do.

TOM: (*Getting awkwardly to his feet*) Oh. Hello. I'm Tom Holloway.

CORALIE: (*To Steve*) You should discuss it with Tom and Lynn. In private. What if you dislike me?

STEVE: It takes time to find that out. What are your feelings? Do you want to discuss it with - erm?

He waves a hand vaguely towards Tony.

CORALIE: I don't think so. It's my decision.

TONY: (*Coldly*) There are one or two things I've noted down that we ought to discuss.

Coralie ignores him. She is staring, fascinated, at Steve.

CORALIE: I imagine you have other people coming to see the room.

Her voice is soft, excluding the others.

STEVE: (*With a grin*) Of course. Hundreds.

CORALIE: (*Slowly*) It would suit me very well.

TONY: (*Aggressively*) In an ideal world, though, the big room next to the kitchen would suit you better.

STEVE: I wondered that. (*Sweetly*) Would you like that room instead?

CORALIE: (*Slowly*) But... that room is... unavailable.

STEVE: Not at all. If you want it, it could be arranged.

There is a tense pause. Lynn stares at Steve in disbelief, Tom with a kind of dumb misery.

STEVE: It would suit you much better - as Terry says.

TONY: Tony.

STEVE: If you like it better why not take it? You've had a good look at it, I presume.

LYNN: (*Icily*) The back room would be more suitable - for all of us. The sound of the clarinet would be further away.

STEVE: (*Airily*) I like the clarinet.

TOM: (*With quiet, bitter intensity, to Steve*) Are you doing this because of - this morning?

STEVE: Of course not. I'm not petty, Tom.

LYNN: (*Sharply, to Coralie*) Don't just stand there. Tell him you don't want to take someone else's room and have them pushed out!

CORALIE: All this has nothing to do with me. I've told you. I shall have nothing to do with any of you. I value my privacy above all else -

LYNN: But you can't come here and encourage Steve to throw Tom out!

A tense pause. Tom did not want her to be as blunt as this.

STEVE: (*Silkily*) Nobody's mentioned throwing Tom out - except you, Lynn darling. Tom, of course, would move into the back room.

LYNN: Oh would he! You snake, Steve.

STEVE: What have I done? Four of us living here. Let's just work out the most amicable way of sharing the rooms. Tom would be very private in the back room. We wouldn't disturb him when he was working. I think you're being a bit hysterical. And I can't for the life of me think why.

LYNN: Perhaps Coralie would like to move into my room? That will be vacant by the weekend! I'm not staying here watching you push people around like puppets - when you're not feeding your face! I'll pay you up to Sunday and not a penny more. You can find somebody else to - to - manipulate!

TOM: *(Stiffly)* There's no need to move out on my account, Lynn.

LYNN: No need! I'm not sharing a flat with a psychopath! I'd rather doss down on Euston Station.

TOM: It's nice of you, Lynn but –

LYNN: You don't know what he's up to. You're not going to put up with his games are you, Tom? You know he's got pints of milk in that 'fridge, don't you? He only took yours to wind you up.

TOM: *(Abruptly)* I can't move out. I haven't got time. It doesn't matter to me where I live, or who I live with. I've got to have somewhere to do my work. *(To Steve)* I'm sorry if I offended you in any way. I'll do whatever you like. I don't mind at all. I need a room to work in. I can't - be disturbed. I'll just fit in with everybody else.

He moves blindly towards the door. Lynn bars his way.

LYNN: Tom. You can't be so - spineless. Don't you realise he won't stop at this?

TOM: I can't afford to be anything else. Let me past please, Lynn. You don't need to go because of me. I don't mind. Really.

He rushes out. There is a pause.

STEVE: You know, Lynn, you should have flounced out earlier. You look just a tinge foolish, having your big gesture flung back in your face. If Tom could be said to do anything as forceful as flinging anything. He's not worth making a big sacrifice for.

LYNN: I'm not going because of Tom. I'm going because of you. I never realised how truly loathsome you really are!

STEVE: *(Icily)* I don't want you to leave, Lynn.

LYNN: Tough.

She crosses to the table, pulls open the paper wrapping the paté, spits into it, then grinds the paper into it, reducing it to a pulpy mess. She drops it into Tom's cornflake bowl.

LYNN: Enjoy your lunch.

She goes out. Steve watches her murderously. Pause.

TONY: *(Jovially)* Well. Good riddance then. Bit of a waste of time her interviewing you wasn't it, Coralie?

But Coralie is staring at Steve. He is still looking after Lynn. Coralie crosses and stands facing him. They look at one another.

CORALIE: How much do you want for *her* room?

They stand quite still, staring at one another. Steve smiles slowly as the lights fade.

THE END

SHADOWS

CHARACTERS

DAVID

PEGGY

NELL

SARAH

The play is set in an empty theatre in the present day.

SHADOWS

A man comes slowly onto the stage, almost feeling his way, as if he is finding his way back to a place he once knew well.

DAVID: Just four short steps... And out of the dark, dusty... private... wings into the light... the limelight. On stage. Moving towards the footlights. The heavy velvet curtain... Red and swagged with gold... rises.

There is the swish of the heavy curtain sweeping up and distant applause.

Looking out over the tiered rows of the audience, in a vast horseshoe encircling me... The red plush seats, shadowy walls and cream and gold mouldings... If I stretch out my hand I feel that I can touch the Grand Circle.

He stretches out his hand and then lets it fall.

No. An empty theatre. A harsh working light. And the ghosts -

A young girl rushes in, flustered and dishevelled. She is carrying a large, floppy bag and an umbrella, which she has put down, and is now shaking vigorously.

PEGGY: Oh, tell me... This is the right place, isn't it? Thank goodness for that. It was so wet I had to get a taxi. Then the taxi driver didn't know where it was - we've been driving around for ages. I was sure I was going to be late.

She has now rid herself of her bag, umbrella etc. And has rubbed her hair dry and brushed the rain off her skirt. She looks round with a mixture of awe and puzzlement.

PEGGY: It's funny isn't it. A theatre like this stuck in the back streets in the middle of all the shops and houses.

DAVID: The theatre was here first.

PEGGY: Where is everybody? Are you the only one - I mean, I thought there'd be more... No. Sorry. Start again. Are you the Director?

DAVID: Director?... Oh no. I hardly think so.

PEGGY: You are here for the audition, aren't you?

DAVID: The audition. That's why you are here?

PEGGY: Yes. I'm here to read for Cordelia. I don't suppose I've got a chance... but it would be wonderful if... I'd be gobsmacked. Actually it's my first real audition. I've just left Drama School.

DAVID: (*Amused*) Where they taught you to be an actress.

PEGGY: Supposed to. Yes. Well.

DAVID: And now you're ready to begin.

PEGGY: Yes. (*Prowling round the stage, looking out at the auditorium.*) I wonder why they're doing the auditions here... There's only going to be six actors. It's a profit-share. Don't suppose there'll be any profits though... But it won't be anywhere like this.

DAVID: **King Lear** with six actors?

PEGGY: Uhuh. Three men and three women.

DAVID: For twenty-one speaking parts. Not to mention the 'Knights attending on Lear, Officers, Messengers, Soldiers and Attendants.'

PEGGY: Yes. I don't know how they'll divide it up.

DAVID: Lear's hundred knights might be a bit of a problem.

PEGGY: It would be lovely to do it here, wouldn't it? I love proper theatres. Especially when they're empty.

DAVID: (*Drily*) Most actors prefer them to be full.

PEGGY: (*Laughing*) Yes. I know. That's not what I mean. Before everybody gets here. It's so quiet... but - alive...

DAVID: Or after they've all gone. Listen. (*Holding up his hand*) You can hear all those generations of players, who have touched hands over the centuries. In an unbroken line, stretching back to Shakespeare himself... Macready acted here. And Ellen Terry, as a young girl, travelling through, on her way to becoming a great actress. And the audiences. If you look out there you can see row upon row of highly proper Victorian ladies and gentlemen - and a few improper ones as well! Respectable matrons with hats and trays of tea at the matinées. Young couples celebrating a night out. Lonely people, forgetting they are alone. Young soldiers in uniform snatching the opportunity to laugh - before they go back -

He stops.

PEGGY: (*Sadly*) The taxi-driver said they're squabbling over it now. The Council wants to pull it down, but it's a listed building. It was a cinema for a bit. Then somebody tried to make a go of it. But they ran out of money...

Pause

DAVID: What are you doing for your audition?

PEGGY: Act 4 Scene 7.

DAVID: Let me see it.

PEGGY: Now?

DAVID: Why not? Here is your stage. Here is your audience.

PEGGY: (*Slightly embarrassed*) Erm. It's the reconciliation with Lear. I've sort of bunched it up together and cut Kent and the Doctor

DAVID: And Lear?

PEGGY: No. Well. I imagine him.

She begins to perform her audition speech. David draws aside and watches her. She mimes her Lear

PEGGY: O my dear father! Restoration hang
Thy medicine on my lips and let this kiss
Repair those violent harms that my two sisters
Have in thy reverence made......
Had you not been their father, these white flakes
Did challenge pity of them. Was this a face
To be oppos'd against the warring winds?
To stand against the deep dread bolted thunder?
In the most terrible and nimble stroke
Of quick cross lightning? to watch - poor perdu!-
With this thine helm? Mine enemy's dog,
Though he had bit me, should have stood that night
Against my fire; and wast thou fain, poor father,
To hovel thee with swine and rogues forlorn,
In short and musty straw? Alack, alack!
'Tis wonder that thy life and wits at once

                    Had not concluded all - He wakes; speak to him...
                    How does my royal lord? How fares your Majesty?
                    David stands quite still where he is and answers her.
DAVID: You do me wrong to take me out o' the grave.
                    Thou art a soul in bliss; but I am bound
                    Upon a wheel of fire, that mine own tears
                    Do scald like molten lead.

PEGGY: Sir, do you know me?

DAVID: You are a spirit, I know. Where did you die?

PEGGY: Still far far wide!

DAVID: Where have I been? Where am I? Fair daylight?
                    I am mightily abus'd. I should e'en die with pity
                    To see another thus. I know not what to say.
                    I will not swear these are my hands. Let's see.
                    I feel this pin prick. Would I were assur'd
                    Of my condition!

PEGGY: O, look upon me, sir,
                    And hold your hands in benediction o'er me.
                    No sir, you must not kneel.

DAVID: Pray, do not mock me
                    I am a very foolish fond old man
                    Fourscore and upward, not an hour more nor less;
                    And to deal plainly,
                    I fear I am not in my perfect mind.
                    Methinks I know you, and know this man;
                    Yet I am doubtful; for I am mainly ignorant
                    What place this is; and all the skill I have
                    Remembers not these garments; nor I know not
                    Where I did lodge last night. Do not laugh at me
                    For as I am a man I think this lady
                    To be my child, Cordelia.

PEGGY: And so I am, I am.

DAVID: Be your tears wet? Yes, faith. I pray weep not;

                    He stops. They look at one another.

PEGGY: Who are you?

DAVID: Just - a jobbing actor.

> *Nell and Sarah rush in. David sidles away, unseen, as they take over the stage, shaking away the rain, tidying themselves up.*

NELL: (*Looking round*) This is a joke isn't it?

SARAH: I am absolutely soaked!

NELL: Why have we had to come all this way? And why on earth have auditions in a great barn like this when we're going to be performing in somebody's spare bedroom?

SARAH: God! This place is like the **Mary Celeste**. Where is everybody? I had an awful job finding it, did you?

NELL: I had to get a taxi. I had a really evil taxi-driver. Never stopped talking and he kept leering at me in the driving mirror. He said he knew this place well. Used to come here regularly years ago. Apparently they used to do strip shows. Very artistic, he said. **Nudes of the World** and **The Nine o'clock Nudes!** Loads of feathers on their heads and they weren't allowed to move. Absolutely years ago. He was about ninety. I was petrified. I think he was far too old to be driving anything faster than a zimmer frame.

SARAH: Well. There's just the three of us then. That ought to be all right.

PEGGY: But where's - ?

SARAH: I want to play Regan of course. You two might clash a bit over Cordelia, I suppose. We must make sure they don't bother to see anybody else.

NELL: (*To Peggy*) I see you as more of a Goneril, really. Don't you?

PEGGY: Where's he gone?

SARAH: Who?

PEGGY: The man. The guy I was… talking to when you arrived.

NELL: Oh him. I thought he was the caretaker.

PEGGY: No. He was - he said he was an actor.

NELL: Amazingly stupid actor. They've cast all the blokes.

SARAH: I suppose he wants to play Cordelia in drag.

NELL: Ugh! Isn't this place awful. It makes me feel itchy. It's filthy. All those ripped seats and falling-down plaster. So dingy... rolls of dust and disgusting rubbish! Look! The rain's got in over there.

SARAH: What's that shuffling noise? Listen!

They listen in horror.

NELL: Mice. Oh... Or rats!

SARAH: As big as cats! Ugh! The sooner we get out of here, the better. Where's this caretaker bloke? We've got to find out what's going on.

PEGGY: He wasn't a caretaker. He said he was an actor.

SARAH: Believe that, you'll believe anything.

NELL: Come on. Let's go and see what we can find. There must be somebody, somewhere. My audition was at 2.30.

SARAH: So was mine.

NELL: Come on then. I'm not going anywhere on my own in this place.

PEGGY: I'll - I'll stay here. In case anyone comes.

SARAH: Suit yourself.

Sarah and Nell go off. Peggy moves to the front of the stage and stretches out her hand wonderingly.

PEGGY: (*Slowly*) 'The best in this kind are but shadows...'

THE END

HELLO, IS THAT YOU?
and
MADAM HAS A COMBINATION SKIN

CHARACTERS

HELLO, IS THAT YOU?

SELINA

MADAM HAS A COMBINATION SKIN

SALLY

HELLO, IS THAT YOU?

We are in a small bed-sitter, a large high-ceilinged room in a Victorian house. In one corner of the room, downstage left, is a divan with a rainbow-coloured bedspread and several brightly coloured cushions piled on it. Right of centre is a large battered armchair. Downstage right is a desk with an angle-poise lamp, several books, files and loose papers on it. The gas fire (imagined) is downstage centre in the 'fourth wall.' A large floor cushion is in front of it. Downstage right of the cushion the telephone stands on a pile of directories. It is late evening.

Selina comes in. She is nineteen, usually lively and outgoing, but at the moment, obviously exhausted and in a state of high nervous tension. She is wearing a large, loose coat which looks as if it has been flung on over her jeans and sweater. Her make-up is smeared and patchy, as if she put it on hours ago, in another existence and has forgotten about it. She comes in carefully, almost as if entering the room for the first time. She stands by the door and talks to herself in a careful half-mutter as if she were talking to someone else. She gives herself a little mental shake and switches on the light by the door. No light comes on.

SELINA: Oh damn!

She goes to the desk and switches on the lamp. Nothing.

Oh no! They can't do this. Not now. Not another power cut.

She goes to the door and calls down the stairs.

Mrs Patecki! Mrs Patecki!

There is no reply. She comes back into the room.

Out. As usual.

She crosses to her desk and takes out a large, heavy duty torch from the drawer. She switches it on and stands it by the 'phone. She sits in the armchair. She is in shadow, a little of the light spilling onto her hands, twisting nervously in her lap. She looks at her watch.

Three minutes to eleven... if the power comes back on by eleven o'clock she'll be all right. (*Pause*) If it doesn't come on till quarter past she'll come out of the coma. If she... Oh, oh! (*Shaking her head painfully*) I'll have to go back to the hospital. I can't sit here in the dark. Why did I come back here? Why didn't I go back home like Mum said? Grandy would have made me some Horlicks in the teddy-bear mug and I would have gone to sleep in my old room... But she would have talked to me - and gone on and on about Mel. And it's closer to the hospital here. Why did Mum send me back now? She thinks Mel's going to die - she doesn't want me there. She let *him* stay though. 'Oh, Selina darling, There's only two beds available. I think Daddy ought to stay - he's come such a long way. And your flat's so close. You could be here in five minutes if...' Why should he stay? He doesn't care about Mel. He just went off with that slag and left us all. He didn't care then. It's all his fault. That's why Mel did it -

Distraught, she jumps up and walks about the room.

No, no, no, it isn't. I didn't say that. You don't try to commit suicide when you're only nine. I didn't mean it, Mel. Please! It - it was an accident. She didn't mean to. She was just in a temper because - because - It wasn't me! It wasn't me. That's what Mum thinks. That's why she sent me away... Please Mel, please, don't die-

The telephone rings. She stares at it, fascinated.

Oh no. Don't let it be the hospital. Oh let them say she's all right!

She kneels on the floor cushion and picks up the 'phone. She is now lit by the torch. The rest of the room a pool of darkness round her.

Hello. Yes... Yes . This is Selina Manders speaking... No. No that's all right, it's not late. I was expecting a call - Who? Gareth.. (*Puzzled*) Gareth? I'm sorry? Oh yes. Joanna's party... last night... Is that when it was? It seems - No, no you wouldn't have got through... I wasn't here this evening... Yes. I remember. I wanted you to 'phone... What?... Yes, that's right this is Selina... We met last night. No I'm fine.. fine...

She stops as if she has no idea where she is or what she is saying. Then suddenly bursts out urgently.

Could you get off the 'phone please! I can't talk to you now... Oh no, look. I'm sorry. I'm sorry. Don't go. Please don't go. I didn't mean to be - It's just that I'm waiting. There might be a 'phone call from the hospital. My sister Melissa's there. She's unconscious, you see. With head injuries. She was in a road accident. (*Breaking down*) No she wasn't. It wasn't an accident. It was my fault. I was horrible to her. She - she's quite plump and I told her she was a disgusting little ball of lard and I was ashamed to be seen with her and she - she - we had a terrible row and she shouted at me, and said she wished she was dead and she might as well kill herself... and she ran out of the house and straight across the road... and there was this van - She didn't mean to do it. And now they're waiting. At the hospital, my Mum and Dad - He doesn't live with us. They're at the hospital and they've sent me home. It's because they know she's going to die and I've killed her. That's what they think. So, I can't talk to you. I would like to see you, but it'll have to wait. Anyway, don't 'phone again. Wait till I... (*Becoming aware that there is no-one there*) Gareth?... Gareth... Gareth?? (*Slowly putting the 'phone down*) I don't know his number. What was his name? Price? Pearce? Gareth Price... No, that wasn't it. Priest? Gareth Priest... It'll be in the book...

The lights suddenly come on. Selina closes her eyes and shakes her head, she blinks and stares at her watch.

Five past eleven. I don't know what that means. If the lights come on at eleven, she'll be all right. If they don't come on till quarter past, she'll come round out of the coma. But I didn't say anything about five past. I didn't -

The 'phone rings. She stares, transfixed, as the lights fade.

THE END

MADAM HAS A COMBINATION SKIN

The sitting room of a small, rather luxurious flat. There is a sofa downstage centre. In front of it stands a coffee table with a telephone and some magazines on it. Somewhere offstage we can hear the persistent beat, and occasional hint of tune, of pop music on the radio being played somewhere behind a closed door.

Sally rushes in upstage right with a make up case and a pile of glossy brochures. She is an energetic, attractive girl in her late teens. At the moment she is very excited and is bursting to tell someone her news.

SALLY: (*As she comes in*) Gemma! Gem! I've got through. I'm definitely going to do it!!

She stops dead in the middle of the room, then crosses and puts the make-up box down on the table and looks round, disappointed.

Oh no!

She crosses downstage left and calls offstage.

Gemma! Are you in that bath again? Come out now! Pleeeease! Oh don't be hours now. I've got loads to tell you... Well... at least turn that radio off.

The music is turned up.

Oh great! Thank you very much. All right - be like that. See if I care. I just won't tell you my fantastic news. You'll be green with envy when you hear. I could even get a trip to New York. Or Paris. (*To herself*) Or it might be Birmingham but we won't think about that.

The music stops.

I thought that would get you... (*Calling out again*) It's fantastically well organized. There were hundreds of girls there. I mean, there were eleven before lunch. I was with them for three quarters of an hour. The girl in front of me was only ten minutes and she was gorgeous looking. But she had a voice like a knife on a window pane. It was terribly plush and

American. Really my sort of thing. Very expensive. You're not just on your own. You're a part of the company... they do you over completely first... they do a colour-coding on your skin type and everything and tell you what colours you should wear - and you mustn't ever wear any other colours when you're at work. And you've got to use their products all the time. You have to have a manicure every week done by them. The first one's free and after that you pay seventy-five per cent... they didn't say how much that comes to... And you mustn't ever wear anything cheap or nasty... Oh do hurry!!! I can't keep shouting through this bathroom door!

There is no reply.

They're going to do a saturation coverage of this area... There's six of us girls. There's these fantastic glossy brochures with free offers in - and they've got a load of school-kids and old age pensioners, or housewives or something delivering them. Then we get a list of all the places they've been to and we phone up and tell them they've won a facial and when will it be convenient for us to call? Then we go round and do the make-over... and we sell them masses of make-up. There's no cheap rubbish. It's really up-market stuff. And we're called **Beauty Philosophers.** We get two days training - in a luxury Hotel and that could be anywhere. I don't know yet where I'll be going. Are you coming out or not? Oh well...

She looks round and crosses to the sofa and sits down, opens the make-up box, takes out a tube of foundation cream and an eyeliner and goes into her routine.

'Hello, I'm Sally. And you're Mrs Smith. May I call you Jean? After all we're going to be very close aren't we? I'm not just here to sell you make-up. I know you don't think that! We leave that to all those door-to-door salesgirls. I'm here to change your life. To give you a new philosophy of life - beauty-wise - (*Dropping the act*) What was that thing they said? Pick on something bad about them and go on about it to make them feel insecure. But be sympathetic. 'Jean, as your beauty friend, I'm going to say this because I think you do a wonderful job - disguising your nose. It's not easy is it? I promise you most people wouldn't even notice - I mean when you've got a double problem - the size *and* the open pores. Do you know some people call it orange peel skin... Isn't that awful? I mean just think of an orange - all those little holes - and don't you think oranges are disgusting to touch? So greasy. And the colour!' (*Remembering*) Oh yes. And pick your own best feature and run it down. Say it's all due to make-up. 'Now Jean, take me. A lot of people say I've got lovely big eyes. It's quite embarrassing they go on about it so much. Because I haven't!! If you saw me without my make-up you'd be amazed. These are pinholes! Absolute pinholes. My eyes are an acquired skill. Do you know you can even do a degree in Beauty Philosophy? **Rose Angel** has founded a School of Beautyology - in America. **Rose Angel** doesn't just change your face she changes your life. Jean - you really want to get rid of those blackheads, don't you? And that teensy- weensy double chin?...' (*Getting up)* Oh God, what if I can't do it? What if they won't even let me in -

The phone rings. She picks it up.

Hello. 9386. Gemma? Oh just a minute. She's in the bath. Gemma! 'Phone! What is it please, can I take a message? ... Oh. (*Very coldly*) No. I'm sorry. I'm afraid Gemma won't want to speak to you. No. I'm absolutely sure... No I won't get her. Because I'm the **Rose Angel** Beauty Philosopher for this area.

She slams the phone down in a fury.

THE END

By the same author

Stage plays

Harvest	Birmingham Repertory Studio Theatre 1980
	Ambassadors Theatre, London 1981
	Samuel French Ltd. 1982
A Lovely Day Tomorrow	Birmingham Repertory Studio Theatre 1983
Anna's Room	Birmingham Repertory Studio Theatre 1984
	Samuel French Ltd. 1985
Weekend Break	Birmingham Repertory Studio Theatre 1985
	The above plays also available in:-
	Harvest & Other Plays.
	First Writes Publications 1996
The Power of the Dog	Orange Tree Theatre, Richmond 1996
	First Writes Publications 1996

Short plays

Natural Causes	Traverse Theatre, Edinburgh 1967
A Good Close Fit	Close Theatre, Glasgow 1969

Musicals

With Don Taylor (Lyrics) and Charles Young (Music)

The Burston Drum	Waterman's Arts Centre 1988
	Samuel French Ltd. 1989
Summer in the Park	Waterman's Arts Centre 1991
	Samuel French Ltd. 1989

First Writes Plays and Playscripts

Ellen Dryden	The Power of the Dog
	Harvest, and Other Plays
Lucy Maurice	Indian Summer
Nicholas McInerny	Red Princess
James Saunders	Retreat
Jack Shepherd	Chasing the Moment
Don Taylor	Retreat from Moscow
	When the Barbarians Came
	The Road to the Sea

First Writes Poetry

Gordon Mason	Stone Circle
Don Taylor	Five Political Poems
	A Prospect of Jerusalem
	Autumn Landscapes

First Writes Books
was originally launched as
First Writes Publications
in Autumn 1994 by
First Writes Theatre Company Ltd.
to publish new plays and poetry.

FIRST
WRITES

Ellen Dryden was born in Whitacre Heath, Warwickshire. Her first full-length stage play, **Harvest**, was premiered at the Birmingham Repertory Theatre and subsequently produced at the Ambassadors Theatre, London. Birmingham Repertory Theatre then commissioned and presented her next three plays **A Lovely Day Tomorrow**, **Anna's Room** and **Weekend Break**.

The Power of the Dog was performed at The Orange Tree Theatre Richmond, in 1996.

She lived and worked in West London until moving to Norfolk in the Autumn of 1995. She was a co-founder and, for ten years, a director of Chiswick Youth Theatre, writing several one-act plays for the young actors, as well as two full-scale musical plays, **The Burston Drum** and **Summer in the Park**.

In 1993, together with Don Taylor and Richard Blake, she formed **First Writes Theatre Company** and continues to work with the company in theatre, publishing and radio.